CODING

PYTHON AND RASPBERRY PI

Author

Larry Lutz and Richard Ray

Python For Beginners

Step-By-Step Guide to Learning Python Programming

Author

Larry Lutz

Table of Contents

Chapter 1

Introduction to Python

Introduction:

The software consists of many small programs interacting with each other. Each program is a combination of instructions in an ordered manner to perform a specific process. Processes are of different types based on the complexity of the program. Development of programs is done based on the type of complexity. Algorithms are needed to find a solution to the problem or implement processes.

An algorithm can be considered as the logic of the program. Each program is written with some type of algorithm. After the development of the program, program testing is done to measure the performance of the program for different inputs. Proper documentation is done with the development of each program for future reference.

To develop any program in the software industry, there are mainly seven stages to follow:

- o Requirement Gathering

- o Analysing problem

- o Decide Input and Output

- o Developing Algorithm

- o Program implementation

- o Testing and Debugging

- o Documentation

To find a solution to any software problem, design approaches play a very important role. It is essential to represent the solution for large complex systems. There are various design approaches evolved over the time in the software domain.

Top-Down Approach:

The system consists of various components in a proper hierarchy. In this design approach, designing is done from top-level components to bottom level components.

Bottom Top Approach:

This is the reverse designing approach to Top-down approach. Bottom Level components are designed first and then move to top-level components. Bottom level components are also called base components of the system.

Modular Approach:

This approach is aimed at segregating the whole system into different modules. Each module is implemented differently using a program. Modules are well defined in terms of input and output, it provides flexibility to modify in future and independent testing. Every language is designed on the basis of its requirement and purpose. Like FORTRAN was developed to solve problems related to science and mathematics, COBOL was developed to find solutions related to business applications.

Python interpreter development was started by Guido van Rossum as his hobby project as a successor to ABC Language, but today because of its simplicity and pseudo code characteristics, it has a million users all around the world. Python interpreter is not only able to solve complex programming problems, but able to target problems of the 21st century in the field of automation, web development, desktop application, and many more.

History:

Python was one of the hobby projects for Guido van Rossum after his regular job in the late 1980s. The irrelevant project name was because of his fondness towards Monty Python's Flying Circus. His intention was to develop a simple and readable code interpreter. Guido released the first version of Python interpreter in the year 1991. Today, there are many python versions available in the series names of 2.X to 3.X and still, latest version are releasing every year.

Presently, Python's development and upgradation are handled by a non-profile organization named Python Software Foundation and Guido van Rossum still holds a very important role in the development of python interpreter. There are many versions of python interpreter, and with every release, its feature has been improved and new features included. In October 2000, Python 2.0 was released.

The major features included were Unicode support and Memory Management with a cyclic-detection garbage collection system. In the year 2008, Python 3.0 was released with major functionalities backward compatibility with python 2.6 and python 2.7 version.

Scripting Language:

- o Python is a high level and general purpose programming language.
- o You might have seen people considering it as a scripting language because they understand script and program as the same.
- o They often use the word "Script" instead of "Program." Python has become the tool for many people around the world because of it's easy to use characteristics. Sometimes Python users also infer "python file" by using the term "script."
- o Commonly, Python is an Object-oriented programming language that inherits all the advantages of OOP and dividing a program into procedures, modules, and functions. Its object-oriented orientation makes it useful for the scripting purpose.

Advantages:

Python language is widely used all over the globe. Its popularity is because of its characteristics and many advantages attached to it. Some of the major advantages are as follows:

Easy-to-Learn, Read and Maintain:

Python's design philosophy focusses more on the readability of the code. Its pseudo code nature makes it easy-to-learn for beginners who want to learn to programme.

Any non-computer science background can understand by reading the code because of its simple English words used as Keywords. Python's code is also very easy-to-maintain.

A handful of Standard Libraries:

Python's package is available with many standard libraries, which are an aid in solving diverse programming challenges. These libraries are also cross-platform compatible. It allows you to port your Python code to any platform such as Windows, Mac, and Linux.

Easy development and Test:

Python Interactive is very popular and a quick Python interpreter. It helps you to test and run code snippets pretty quick. When you are in the middle of a large program and need to test some code, you just need to run Python interpreter and run into it.

Graphical User Interface programming:

Python avails many libraries for the development of GUI such as Tkinter, Wx, and PyQt, etcetera. These libraries support system calls and cross-platform compatibility.

Extendable to Low-Level languages:

Python also allows you to include low-level programming modules like C, C++, and Java in your code that aid in the development of efficient and fast solutions. Because of its extendable nature, you can have all the advantages of a low-level programming language with quick development.

Disadvantages:

With the numerous advantages of using the Python language over the year in various fields. there are also some downsides of using it for some applications.

o Python is a high-level language, so its execution speed is not as fast as compared to C and C++. But over time, Python libraries are optimized to use it in applications where timing is the important aspect.

o For GUI programming, Python libraries are optimized enough to provide service almost as fast as C and C++.

Exercise

1. Explain the design philosophy of Python.

    Answer: Guido had the following philosophy while designing and implementing:

    - Python's implementation should not be tied to a specific platform. There is no problem if some features are not always available, but the core should work anywhere.

    - Do not disturb the details the machine handles.

    - Mistakes should not be fatal. That is, as long as the virtual machine is still valid, the user code should be able to recover from the error condition.

    - The user's Python code should not be allowed to cause errors in the Python interpreter's undefined behavior; the core dump will never be the user's fault.

2. What are the key features in python?

   Answer: Key features of python is as following –

   - Python is an interpreted language. This means that, unlike C and its variant languages, Python does not need to be compiled before it runs. Other interpreted languages include PHP and Ruby.

   - In Python, a function is a first class object. This means that it is assigned to a variable, returned from another function, and passed to the function. The class is also a first class object.

   - The creation of Python code is fast, but it runs slower than the compiled language.

   - Python is suitable for object-oriented programming. This is to enable class definitions, combinations, and inheritance.

   - Python offers applications in many areas, including web applications, automation, scientific modelling, and large-scale data applications. It is also often used as a "glue" code to make differences in other languages and components.

Chapter 2

Utilities of Python

Introduction:

Based on the various statistics available online, there are almost a million users of the Python language. The numerical data may be more or less than that as Python is open source language and this data is probably based on the number of downloads. Python source code is available online, but Python Software Foundation still holds Copy-rights for this language.

Python's source code is available to use under GNU General Public License. Today, Python package comes pre-installed with Macintosh and Linux operating system. Because of its various impactful characteristics, Python is used in many software solutions and applied to solve real-time problems with profit generating solutions.

Big giants like Google, Netflix, and Dropbox have used the Python language in many ways. The backend process of

Google web search engine is written in Python. The world's largest collection of videos, Youtube, is completely developed in Python. The Dropbox used Python in storage services and for its desktop applications.

Utilities

Besides the well-designed characteristics of Python, Python is used to solve many real-world problems in the various domains. Programmers also use it for solving their day-to-day life problems. In fact, Python applications are nearly unlimited as it can be used from simple gaming applications to high-end complex aerospace and robotics solutions.

Some of the present and emerging applications as described in the following sections:

Graphical User Interface:

Python has a rich set of GUI libraries that could be used developing front-end for applications. These GUIs are supported by Macintosh, Windows, and Linux distributions. Tk library is included automatically with Python 2.0 named Tkinter. This library could also be extended by PMW library to use enhanced widgets in front-end. Qt GUI library is also available with name PyQt and Swing GUI with name Jython. These GUIs are not only available limited to computer applications, but also in embedded applications.

Web-Scripting:

Python has made the complex client-server programming really very simple by the use of standard libraries available with it. These modules let programmers to implement networking task pretty quick. Python scripts also help in creating sockets and data communication over it. File transferring using FTP and parsing XML data is easy-to-implement. There are available methods for network communications for sending, receiving, parsing, and creating e-mails.

Database Programming:

For the demand of accessing the data from the database traditionally, Python also avails features of database accessing and programming for the commonly used databases like MySQL, Oracle, ODBC, and Sybase. It is also considered as the portable database API as it provides the code portability for database just by changing vendor interface.

Mathematical and Scientific Applications:

Python is able to target problems of complex math as well as scientific domain that has not been targeted by any programming language traditionally. NumPy is the very popularly used numeric library, which allows the programmer to solve quick numeric problems in programming application. It is one of the Python's compelling utilities.

There are many more standard libraries available for numeric computations and representation of numeric data in 3-D plot models. SciPy and ScientificPython are popular libraries used as scientific tools that differentiate Python from the other traditional programming languages. These are well optimized in terms of processing the complex algorithms and math. Due to this reason. NumPy is the core interface in the development of SciPy library.

Gaming Application:

Gaming software industries also take advantage of Python libraries such as PyGame, PySoy, Pyglet, and others. Some libraries also include multimedia functionalities with it.

Embedded Applications:

Embedded is a combination of software and hardware component such as microprocessor and microcontroller based applications. Raspberry pi is one such popular microprocessor which uses the Python language for the firmware development. All the modules that control it are written in the Python language.

Image and Data-Mining Applications:

Image processing and Data-mining are the emerging fields in the 21st century. There are various interfaces available that are being used for image processing applications like PyOpenGL, OpenCV, and Maya. Data-mining deals with the large set of data and applying mathematical calculations for generating results, and Python is a great tool for the same. Matplotlib and Mayavi are the common interfaces available modules for data mining and visualization.

Exercise

1. What is the difference between deep and shallow copy?

   Answer:

Shallow copy: When creating a new instance type, use shallow copy and keep the value copied to the new instance. Shallow copies are used to copy reference pointers in the same way as copy values. These references point to the original object, and changes to the members of the class will also affect the original copy. Using shallow copies reduces program execution time and depends on the size of the data used.

Deep copy: Deep copy is used to store the copied values. With deep copy, reference pointers to objects are not copied. It contains a reference to an object and a new object pointed to by another object. Changes made to the original copy do not affect the use of other copies of the object. Deep replication slows program execution because copies of each invoked object are created.

2. Explore more utilities of Python programming language.

   Answer: Many organizations are currently using Python to perform key tasks. Organizations usually have information to publish trade secrets, so you do not necessarily need to listen to these messages. However, Python plays an important role in organizing the way we work and maintain revenue. Here are some of the key ways companies can use Python. This makes Python easier to use in your organization.

   - Corel
   - D-Link
   - Eve – Online
   - Forecast watch
   - Frequentis
   - HP

- Honeywell

Chapter 3

Configuring Python Environment

Before you start with the Python programming, you need Python on your computer. You can check whether Python is already installed on your computer or not. Open your command line windows and type "python" and hit enter, if it displays any response from Python interpreter with the version number then you don't need to download Python on your system.

Python is available on wide variety of platforms. You can download Python for all different environments and it can be ported to the Java and .net virtual machines. For example, you can use python on your UNIX, Linux, Windows, Macintosh, DOS, etcetera.

Getting python:

The most up to date and previous version of Python is available on the official Python website with source code, binaries, and all preferable documentation. You can visit the official Python website at https://www.python.org/.

You can download or refer Python documents from https://www.python.org/doc/. The particular documentation is available for all versions of Python.

Installing Python:

Python is available for wide variety of platforms. You need to download the binary file of Python version according to the platform and then install Python on your computer.

If the binary code is not available for your platform, then you can use a C compiler to compile the source code manually. Compilation of source code gives more flexibility in terms of choice of features.

Windows Installation:

Python interpreter is not pre-installed in Windows, but it does not mean that Windows users won't find a useful, flexible programming language. However, installing the latest version of Python is not a trivial matter, so you make sure to find the right tool for the task.

You can download latest version of Python 2 and Python 3 according to your need. The installer will install 32-bit or 64-bit version according to your computer automatically.

Python 2 Installation:

You can install Python 2 version from the official Python site https://www.python.org/downloads/. The latest version is also available but if you want to download an older version then you can do it by downloading its binary code. Click on Download Python 2.7.14 so it will start downloading binary code on your computer automatically.

- While downloading, the installer will set a path variable for you. Download and Run the installer.

Looking for a specific release?

Python releases by version number:

Release version	Release date		Click for more
Python 3.6.4	2017-12-19	⬇ Download	Release Notes
Python 3.6.3	2017-10-03	⬇ Download	Release Notes
Python 3.3.7	2017-09-19	⬇ Download	Release Notes
Python 2.7.14	2017-09-16	⬇ Download	Release Notes
Python 3.4.7	2017-08-09	⬇ Download	Release Notes
Python 3.5.4	2017-08-08	⬇ Download	Release Notes
Python 3.6.2	2017-07-17	⬇ Download	Release Notes

View older releases

- Select Install for all users and click on Next button.

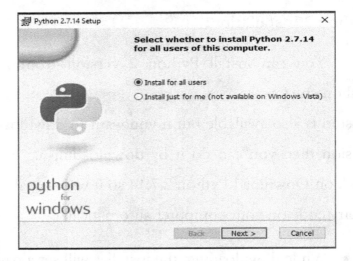

- While selecting the directory, leave the directory as Python 27 and click on Next button.

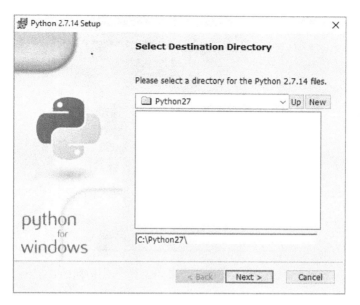

- On customize Python screen, click on "Add python.exe to path" and then select the option "Will be installed on local hard drive." After selecting option, click on Next button.

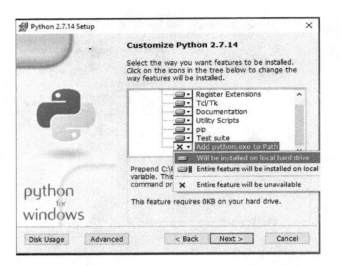

- After clicking on Next, it will start the installation process. After completing it, click on Finish button.

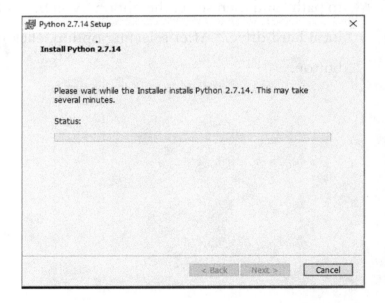

- You can search for python in "Start" Menu and can open Python Idle and Python Command line for more operation.

You can install and work on both Python version 2 and 3 simultaneously on your system. But when you type "Python" at the command prompt, it will point to Python 2.7.

It is because of the variable pointing to the directory and all executable present in that directory that works as the command in the command line. If two directories are present and both have a "python.exe" file, then it will use a variable of the directory which is higher in the list. If there is variable for user and system then system path takes precedence over user path.

To remove it, you can change the name of Python folder, "python" for Python 2 and "python3" for Python 3 in the directory where you have installed Python on the computer. After changing the name in the installed directory you can check version in the command line.

If you are not satisfied with this solution, then you can reorder the environment variable and use Python version according to the need of your project.

Linux Installation:

You can install and setup Python by using Terminal, which is non-graphical. Instead of selecting options from GUI screen and click on buttons, you need to write commands and receive feedback from your computer.

Ubuntu 16.04 comes with the Python 2 and Python 3 pre-installed. To make sure that you have the latest version of Python or not, you can update and upgrade your computer with apt-get command.

$ sudo apt-get update

$ sudo apt-get –y upgrade

The -y flag will confirm that you are installing all the projects in the system, but depending on your Linux version, you need to select additional prompts during system updates and upgrades.

If you are using an older version of Ubuntu and other Linux based operating systems in which Python is not pre-installed, then you can use the following command for installing Python:

$ sudo apt-get install python2.7

You can check the version of installed Python by typing the command:

$ python2.7 –V

You will receive output with the Python version in the terminal window. The output will look like this:

Python 2.7.14

To install pip in your system, use command:

$ sudo apt-get install –y python-pip

Macintosh Installation:

The installation process of Python is somewhat similar in the Linux and Macintosh. Macintosh comes with the pre-installed Python version. You can check the version of Python by typing:

$ python –V or

$ python --version

If you are installing Python again or need to install the latest version of Python, then you need to type the following command:

$brew install python

Python IDEs:

There are many Python IDE (Integrated Development Environment) that are useful for you to work on a Python project. IDE can easily handle big projects that have hundreds of small modules. The main focus while working on IDE is on simplicity and ease of use. It provides a graphical interface to the programmer for their ease. Some of them are very lightweight and fast while working on Python projects. Here is the list of IDEs which are compatible with Windows, Linux, and Mac:

- IDLE
- PyDev
- Eric
- LiClipse
- NetBeans
- Pycharm
- Pyscripter
- Spyder
- Python tools for Visual Studio

There are some of the IDEs which comes with the integrated GUI builder. It is useful when you are working on any Python based GUI projects. They are:

- MonkeyStudio
- Xcode
- Visual Python
- PythonCard

Exercise

1. Install the Python package in your system. Refer to the steps as your operating system specified in the chapter.

Chapter 4

Basics of Python

In the previous chapter, we have learned about the various characteristics, utilities, and configuration of Python in your systems. Now it's the time to start with the understanding of the basic Python scripts and get familiar with the programming environment of it.

We will be using the Linux distribution environment for writing and running the scripts throughout this book. You can use any environment other than Linux such as Macintosh or Windows and configure your Python package as explained in the previous chapter and get set go.

Hello, World Program

Hello, World is the most basic program to learn any computer programming language with. Python is a really quick and dirty programming language. It's just a matter of time that you have any solution in your mind and you quickly code it, thanks to the pseudo-code design philosophy of python.

You can either use Python Interactive Mode to write your first Hello, World program and it will provide a prompt output or by using the traditional method for writing program in a text editor. Here both ways have been explained:

Let's get started,

By using Text Editor:

Open any of your favourite text editor such as Notepad, VI editor, or VIM etcetera. Write the following program in it and save it with the name "helloWorld.py".

$ print "Hello, World"

```
# Hello World Program
print "Hello, World!!"
```

To run the program, you need to open Terminal (in Linux) or Command line window (in Windows). Change your current directory to the program file folder and run following command:

$ python helloWorld.py

The output is as follows:

```
Hello, World!!
```

By using Python Interactive:

Python Interactive is a mode of python which programmers use to write a quick code snippet and test it while working with the large programs. The significance and utility of Python Interactive is explained more in-depth in coming section of this chapter.

Here you can just have a hands-on experience of Python Interactive with this example.

Let's start with it. Open Terminal in your system and Type following:

$ python

```
Python 2.7.12 (default, Nov 19 2016, 06:48:10)
[GCC 5.4.0 20160609] on linux2
Type "help", "copyright", "credits" or "license"
>>> ▮
```

With this command, you are calling Python interpreter to run in interactive mode. Write following one line Hello, World program and then press Enter.

% >>> print "Hello, World"

With the Enter button, promptly it will display output as following:

```
>>> print "Hello, World"
Hello, World
```

This method of running your Hello, World program is just for your experience with Python Interactive. To write any further programs, we will be using traditional text editor method.

Let's understand more in-detail about the steps and the program that we have run.

To get a brief of the one-liner program. Break it into two parts: one is print and the other one is "Hello, World." Print is a function call, similar to the printf function in C. It displays data to output screen in string form and "Hello, World" is a string which is an argument to print function. As of now, you should not think too much about strings and function. These are explained well in the following chapters.

Python Interactive:

The interactive window of Python is simple and also very useful for the programmer during the development of Python code. It is similar to sitting in-front of Python interpreter and getting results for each Python expression. This aids programmers in experimenting and testing of code snippets.

To wake up Python interactive mode in your system, you just need to type Python and hit enter in Terminal. It will next display a few lines with details of python interpreter like version number and others and prompt your for input with ">>>" As showing in the following:

```
Python 2.7.12 (default, Nov 19 2016, 06:48:10)
[GCC 5.4.0 20160609] on linux2
Type "help", "copyright", "credits" or "license" for more information.
>>> █
```

When you work with Python interactively, it will give the result of each expression in the next line as you type it and press Enter key. Due to this, it is not required for you to put a print command in Python interactive mode. Here in the following expression: x = 10, which represents x is assigned with integer value 10 and on pressing Enter key, its value is being displayed. Similarly for str = "Hello, World". The string "Hello, World" is assigned to str variable.

```
>>> str = "Hello, World"
>>> str
'Hello, World'
```

Now It is certainly clear the reason behind the use of Python interactive mode. Being a smart programmer, you can experiment with a few lines of Python commands to see the behaviour of Python when working with large programs.

Basic Built-in Function:

Python package is available with several useful input-output functions. Being a beginner Python programmer, it is a must to understand and remember these functions. These functions' names, syntax, and descriptions are as following:

1. raw_input() or input() :

    This function is similar to the scanf function in C. It is used to take input from the user.

2. print():

This function is useful for printing the data to the output windows in string form.

3. len():

This function is used to get the length of the object. Here the object can be a string, a tuple, or a list and the object is passed as an argument in the len function.

4. str():

This function is useful for converting the type of object. Object version is changed to string type.

5. abs()

This is a mathematical function and it is same as the absolute maths function. It provides the absolute value of the object.

6. help()

This function is very useful for getting information of any function, method or keyword. If no object is passed in the function, It will prompt to a Python help window, and if any string is passed through it as an object, then it will search for that string in the documentation and shows relevant function or data.

7. min():

This function gives the smallest element in an iterative object or it will give the smallest element when multiple objects are passed.

8. max()

this function gives the largest element in an iterative object or it will give the largest element when multiple objects are passed.

9. all()

This function returns a Boolean value that is either True or False. It gives True as the return value when all the elements in the iterative object elements are true.

10. any():

This function also returns a Boolean value. It gives True as a return value when any of the elements in the iterative object elements are true.

Exercise

1. Create and Run a program to display following string text.

   "python is widely used programming language"

   Code:

   ```
   print "python is widely used programming language";
   ```

   Output:

   ```
   python is widely used programming language
   ```

2. Create a python program to take input string from the user and display it on output window.

   Code:

   ```
   str = raw_input("Enter string: ");
   print "input is: ", str
   ```

Output:

```
Enter string: Hello python
input is:  Hello python
```

Chapter 5

Variables, String and Operators

Variables are the identifier which reserve location in the memory to store values. It means when you are creating any variable, it is creating some space in the memory.

The interpreter will allocate memory based on the data type of variable, and data type defines the type of value the variable holds. The variables can hold integer, character, string, and other data types

Variables(Values):

A value is a small unit of the program like letter and number, which is used while assigning to the variable. We don't need to declare a variable before assigning value. Python interpreter will automatically assign the type of data while assigning the value to that variable.

The = sign is used for assignment. The left part of the equal sign is a variable and right part of the equal sign is a value which is assigned to that variable.

Code:

```
name = "Mark"
height =6
age = 25

print (name)
print (height)
print (age)
```

Output:

```
Mark
6
25
```

In the above code, the variables are "name", "age", and "height" and we are assigning the values to each variable. The variable name is storing the character values, age is storing integer value, and height is storing the float value. We don't need to declare the data type of variable; it will automatically assign data type according to the assigned values.

Rules for variable name:

- The variable name must start with an underscore or character.

- The variable name is case-sensitive and contains only alphanumeric character.

- The variable name can't contain any spaces.

- You can't use reserved words as a variable name.

Data Types:

A variable can hold different types of data in the memory. For storing a name, a string is used, age in numeric value, height in float value. There are some standard data types in Python programming language that you can use for storing data in the memory.

These are the standard data types are:

- String
- Tuple
- Dictionary
- Numbers

- List

Strings:

In the Python language, a string is a sequence of text and bytes. A string starts with a single and double quote. You can also use single quotes within double quotes and vice versa.

In simple words, a string is an array of characters and you can use indexing to access the elements of an array. The index starts at 0 on the left and -1 on the right. In Python, strings are immutable in nature. You cannot change character in string once it is generated. The 'in' operator is used when we need to check presence of substring in the string. The result of matching the string is represented in the form of Boolean value.

Python provides us the very simple method to cut the substring from a string. It is known as string slicing. You can separate two indices by the colon (:).

How to access string Values?

Python language does not support character datatype because the character is treated as a string in Python. It gives a length of string and hence it is considered as a substring.

Code:

```
char1 = 'Hello Python'
str1 = "Python Programming"
print ("First value is: " , char1)
print ("Second value is: ", str1)
```

Output:

```
('First value is: ', 'Hello Python')
('Second value is: ', 'Python Programming')
```

Update String:

Reassigning an existing string with new string will give you updated string. The new string can be related to the previous string or completely new string.

Code:

```
char = "Hello Python"
print ("New String is: " , char)
```

Output:

```
('New String is: ', 'Hello Python')
```

Escape Character:

Backslash Notation	Description
\a	Alert
\b	Backspace
\cx	Control X
\e	Escape
\f	Form feed
\n	New line
\r	Carriage return
\s	Space
\t	Tab
\v	Vertical Tab

Tuples:

A tuple is another type of data type which consists of series of comma- separated values. Like strings, tuples are also immutable and enclosed in the parenthesis with holding mix data type. Like strings, tuples can also be sliced. When we slice tuple, it will create a new tuple, but it does not change the original tuple. Addition(+) Operator is used to create a new tuple that is concatenation of more than two tuples. We use * operator to repeat a tuple.

Code:

```
tuple = ('python', 465, 'language', 70.8)
tuple1 = (458, 'program')

print tuple
print tuple[1]
print tuple[1:2]
print tuple[2: ]
print tuple1 * 2
print tuple + tuple1
```

Output:

```
('python', 465, 'language', 70.8)
465
(465,)
('language', 70.8)
(458, 'program', 458, 'program')
('python', 465, 'language', 70.8, 458, 'program')
```

Dictionary:

In the Python language, dictionary data type is like a hash table. It works like an associative array and hashes similar to Perl. Basically, it consists of key-value pairs. A dictionary key is generally a number and a string but it can be of any Python data type. The values can be like arbitrary Python object.

Code:

```
dictionary = {}
dictionary['one'] = "This is one"
dictionary[2] = "This is two"
dictionary1 = {'name': 'Mark', 'EID' : 4578, 'dept' : 'marketing'}
print dictionary['one']          # Print values for 'one' key
print dictionary[2]              # Print value for key 2
print dictionary1                # Print complete dictionary
print dictionary.keys()          # Print all key
print dictionary.values()        # Print all values
```

Output:

```
This is one
This is two
{'dept': 'marketing', 'name': 'Mark', 'EID': 4578}
[2, 'one']
['This is two', 'This is one']
```

Numbers:

The Number data type is used to store numerical values like 1, 2, etcetera. It is used when programmers need to assign a numeric value to the variable. For example,

age = 25

height = 6

Del is used when you want to delete a single or multiple objects. For example,

del age

del age, height

Generally, there are four types of numeric value that you can use in python :

- int (signed integer)
- long (it can be represented in octal and hexadecimal)
- float (floating point values)
- complex

Basic Operator:

The operators are symbols which are used to perform mathematical and logical operations. Operands are the values on which the operator is applied while operations.

Types of Operators:

- Assignment operator

- Logical operator

- Arithmetic operator

- Relational operator

- Bitwise operator

- Identify operator

- Membership operator

Arithmetic Operator:

Symbol	Operator Name
+	Addition
-	Subtraction
*	Multiplication
/	Division
%	Modulus
**	Exponent
//	Floor Division

Logical Operator:

Symbol	Operator Name
or	Logical OR
and	Logical AND
Not	Logical NOT

Assignment Operator:

Symbol	Operator Name
=	Equal
+=	Add AND
-+	Subtract AND
*=	Multiply AND
/=	Division AND
%=	Modulus AND
**=	Exponent AND
//=	Floor Division AND

Relational Operator:

Symbol	Operator Name
==	Double Equal
!= or <>	Not Equal To
>	Greater Than
<	Less Than
<=	Less Than Equal To
>=	Greater Than Equal To

Bitwise Operator:

Symbol	Operator Name
&	Binary AND
|	Binary OR
^	Binary XOR

~	Binary 1s Complement
<<	Binary Left Shift
>>	Binary Right Shift

Identity Operator:

Symbol	Operator Name
Is	Is
Is not	Is not

Membership operator:

Symbol	Operator Name
In	In
Not in	Not in

Exercise

1. Explain Variable and write a code using it.

Answer: Variables are the identifier which reserve memory location to store values. It means when you are creating any variable, it is creating some space in the memory.

Code:

```
name = "Mark"
height =6
age = 25

print (name)
print (height)
print (age)
```

Output:

```
Mark
6
25
```

2. Explain Strings and write a code using it.

Answer: A string is a sequence of text and bytes. A string starts with a single and double quote. You can also use single quotes within double quotes and vice versa.

Code:

```
char1 = 'Hello Python'
str1 = "Python Programming"
print ("First value is: " , char1)
print ("Second value is: ", str1)
```

Output:

```
('First value is: ', 'Hello Python')
('Second value is: ', 'Python Programming')
```

3. Explain Operators and name different types of Operators?

Answer: The operators are symbols which are used to perform mathematical and logical operations. Operands are the values on which the operator is applied while in operations.

Types of Operators:

- Assignment operator
- Logical operator
- Arithmetic operator
- Relational operator
- Bitwise operator

- Identify operator

- Membership operator

Chapter 6

Mathematical Aspects

Introduction:

Mathematics is one of the integral parts of programming. Be it a simple maths operation or writing a complex mathematical algorithm for software, python is always ahead in terms of its speed and quick coding practices. Mathematical data is taken as the data object in the Python language. In fact, objects are the building block of Python programming. We will be learning the usage of basic mathematical functions which are frequently used during Python programming. There are many popular and optimized mathematics and scientific libraries available, which are either built-in or can be imported into your Python code to use.

Basic Mathematics Operations:

In addition to the simple operation like addition (+), subtraction (-), multiplication (*), and division(/), there are many mathematical functions available in Python. As the new versions of Python releases, more mathematical functions are added to the package. In Python version 2.7, there are many methods available in the math library such as numeric theoretical functions, power and logarithmic functions, trigonometric and hyperbolic function, and some special functions.

Code:

```
"""
Program to peform basic arithmatic operation
"""
num1 = int(raw_input("Enter Input 1 :"))
num2 = int(raw_input("Enter Input 2 :"))

print "Addition is %d" % (num1 + num2)
print "Subtraction is %d" % (num1 - num2)
print "Multiplication is %d" % (num1*num2)
print "Division is %d" % (num1/num2)
```

Output:

```
Enter Input 1 :45
Enter Input 2 :78
Addition is 123
Subtraction is -33
Multiplication is 3510
Division is 0
```

In the following sections, we will look more into its usage and prototype:

70

1. Numeric-theoretic Functions:

This module already comes with a built-in Python version 2.7. It is similar to C math library. These functions take one or two objects as data, but it does not take any complex number as objects. Cmath is another Python librarycmath, which is available for complex number math operations.

math.ceil(a) : This function is the same as the ceil function in mathematics. It provides ceil value of 'a' with float datatype. It is the smallest integer value which is greater than or equal to 'a'.

math.floor(a): This function is same as the floor function in mathematics. It provides floor value of 'a' with float datatype. It is the largest integer value which is less than or equal to 'a'.

math.factorial(a) : It returns factorial value of 'a', where 'a' is a positive and integer data, otherwise, it throws an error.

math.fabs(a) : This function returns absolute value of 'a'.

math.copysign(a, b): This function is used to change the sign of the number. It returns data of 'a' with the sign of 'b'.

Let's understand above functions further with Python programming. In the below program:

Code:

```
"""
Program to perform math function
"""
import math

a = 1.456

print "Ceil value of a is %d" % math.ceil(a)
print "Floor value of a is %d" % math.floor(a)
print "Absolute value of a is %d" % math.fabs(a)

b = 5
c = -5
print "Factorial of b is %d" % math.factorial(b)
print "Copied Sign value of b is %d" % math.copysign( b, c)
```

Output:

```
Ceil value of a is 2
Floor value of a is 1
Absolute value of a is 1
Factorial of b is 120
Copied Sign value of b is -5
```

In addition to the above function, a few more functions are available in Python. You can have a look at the python documentation for more.

2. Power and Logarithmic Functions:

Python provides following functions in this category:

math.pow(a,b): This function returns 'a' raised to the power of 'b, where both the data objects should have valid data. For invalid data, the function throws an error.

math.sqrt(a): This function returns square root value of 'a'.

math.log10(a): This function returns logarithmic value of 'a', where the base of the logarithm is 10.

math.log1p(a): This function returns natural logarithmic value of 'a', where base of logarithm is e (constant)

math.exp(a): This function returns exponential value of 'a'

Code:

```
"""
Program to peform math functions.
"""
import math

a = 10
b = 2

print "Power of a raised to b :%d" % math.pow( a, b)
print "Square root of a :%d" % math.sqrt(a)
print "Logarithmic Value of a(base-10) :%d" % math.log10(a)
print "Logarithmic Value of a(base-e)  :%d" % math.log1p(a)
print "Exponential of a :%d" % math.exp(a)
```

Output:

```
Power of a raised to b :100
Square root of a :3
Logarithmic Value of a(base-10) :1
Logarithmic Value of a(base-e)  :2
Exponential of a :22026
```

3. Trigonometric and Hyperbolic Functions:

Python has all trigonometric and hyperbolic functions available in its package. These functions' returns value in radian unit and functions same as the mathematics trigonometric and hyperbolic function.

<u>Trigonometric:</u>

math.sin(a)

math.cos(a)

math.tan(a)

<u>Hyperbolic:</u>

math.sinh(a)

math.cosh(a)

math.tan(a)

Code:

```
"""
Program to perform trigonimetric function
"""
import math

a = 10

print "Sine of a :%f" % math.sin(a)
print "Cosine of a :%f" % math.cos(a)
print "Tan of a :%f" % math.tan(a)
print "Hyperbolic Sine of a :%f" % math.sinh(a)
print "Hyperbolic Cosine of a :%f" % math.cosh(a)
print "Hyperbolic Tan of a :%f" % math.tanh(a)
```

Output:

```
Sine of a :-0.544021
Cosine of a :-0.839072
Tan of a :0.648361
Hyperbolic Sine of a :11013.232875
Hyperbolic Cosine of a :11013.232920
Hyperbolic Tan of a :1.000000
```

4. Special Functions:

Other than the standard maths functions, Python also provides special mathematical functions. They are as following:

math.gamma(a):

This function returns mathematics gamma function value of 'a'.

math.lgamma(a):

This function is a combination of natural logarithm and gamma function. First, it finds the gamma function value at 'a', and then returns natural logarithmic value of absolute value of the result.

math.erf(a):

This function returns error function value at 'a'.

math.erfc(a):

> This function returns complementary error function value at 'a'.

Till now, we have discussed the basic mathematics function. Python is also rich with its advanced mathematical capabilities. Its richness also attracted people from research and scientific backgrounds. NumPy, SciPy, and Matplotlib are very well contained and optimized libraries. Every Python programmer must be well versed with these libraries to enhance their Python programming skills. We will learn more in-depth about these libraries and its utilities.

NumPy Library :

NumPy is a short name for Numeric or Numerical Python and developed as the open source project by Travis Oliphant. The key idea behind the development of this library was to handle multi-dimensional data (array) in Python. It was developed by merging two predecessor libraries, one is Numeric and another is Numarray.

NumPy has power to process multi-dimensional array at fast speed. There are following operations you can perform using NumPy.

1. Logical and mathematical operations on multi-dimensional data or matrix.
2. Linear algebra and generating random numbers.
3. Fourier transforms.

Usually, this library won't be pre-installed with your Python package. You need to install it separately using Pip Python module using the following command in Terminal.

$ pip install numpy

There are following methods and functions which are available in NumPy library.

1. Numpy.zeros(a,b,c)

   The function creates a new array with all elements entries as zero. Where

   'a' is the shape of new array or size of array.

   'b' is the datatype for the elements and, it is optional.

   'c' is the order of array and it is also optional.

2. Numpy.ones(a,b,c)

> This function creates a new array with all elements entries as one and data objects are same as of zeros function.

3. Numpy.full(a,b,c,d)

> This function returns a newly created array and provides shape and value where

> 'a' is the shape of new array or size of array.

> 'b' is the value to be fill in the array.

> 'c' is the datatype for the elements, and it is optional.

> 'd' is the order of the array, and it is also optional.

Code:

```
"""
Program to perform numpy function
"""
import numpy

# 1-d array of zeros
arr1 = numpy.zeros(5)
print "arr1 :"
print arr1

# 2-d array of zeros
arr2 = numpy.zeros((3,2))
print "arr2 :"
print arr2


# 1-d array of ones
arr3 =  numpy.ones(3)
print "arr3 :"
print arr3

# 2-d array of ones
arr4 =  numpy.ones((2,3))
print "arr4 :"
print arr4

# array of any scalar value
arr5 = numpy.full(5, 10)
print "arr5 :"
print arr5
```

Output:

```
arr1 :
[0. 0. 0. 0. 0.]
arr2 :
[[0. 0.]
 [0. 0.]
 [0. 0.]]
arr3 :
[1. 1. 1.]
arr4 :
[[1. 1. 1.]
 [1. 1. 1.]]
arr5 :
[10 10 10 10 10]
```

SciPy Library :

SciPy name stands for Scientific Python. It is an extension of Python NumPy library to enhance its processing and algorithmic capabilities. As NumPy provides methods for creating multi-dimensional data and its processing in Python, SciPy is one step ahead. It is specifically built for implementation of scientific processing like writing mathematical algorithms application. Because of it, Python is a perfect language if you are programming for niche applications such as scientific, web, and desktop applications.

For installing SciPy in your system, you need following commands in your Terminal window.

```
$ sudo apt -get install python-scipy
```

SciPy library is structured into various sub-packages and each sub-package is specific to particular computing domain. These sub-packages and their computing domains are as following :

1. constants: Mathematical Constants.

2. Fftpack: Fast Fourier transform functions.

3. Interpolate: Interpolation functions.

4. Cluster: Clustering algorithms functions.

5. Io: Input and Output.

Before using any sub-package function in your program. You need to import library, for example:

$ from SciPy import constants, io

It is time to go deep into the SciPy library, We will understand some basic functions one-by-one and quickly program it. Let's get started:

1. Constants: The SciPy contains various constant values which are used in both scientific and mathematical calculations. Constants like c (Speed of Light), h (Plank's constant), e (elementary Charge), etcetera.

2. Fftpack: In signalling related applications Fftpack is vastly used. There are many transforming functions present in it.

fft(x[, n, axis, overwrite_x): It is used for generating discrete Fourier transform of any real or complex sequence.

Ifft(x[, n, axis, overwrite_x): It is used for generating discrete inverse Fourier transform of any real or complex sequence.

fft2(x[, shapes, axis, overwrite_x): It is used for finding 2-dimensional Fourier transform.

Ifft2(x[, shapes, axis, overwrite_x): It is used for finding 2-dimensional inverse Fourier transform.

3. Interpolate: In this domain, functions related to various mathematical interpolation methods are available. These functions and their descriptions are as follows:

Interp1d(x,y[,kind,axis,copy,...]): It is used for interpolation of one-dimensional function.

KroghInterpolator(xi,yi[,axis]): It is used for interpolation of a set of points.

4. Cluster: Clustering is one of the latest methods you can use in information theory, compression of data, and detection of the targets. Further, the cluster subpackage contains two modules. One is vq and another is hierarchy. Vq is particularly used for vector quantisation and K-mean algorithm. Hierarchy module supports hierarchical clustering.

5. Io: SciPy supports reading from files and writing to files in various formats. It could be any data like text, numeric, or binary. You can use file like Matrix Market file, Matlab file, IDL files, etcetera.

Code:

```
"""
Program to perform scipy function
"""

import scipy, numpy
from scipy import interpolate

# Constant values
print "Value of e :" + str(scipy.e)

# fftpack
y  = scipy.fft([1.0, 2.0, 3.0, 1.5])
print "Fast Fourier Transform of y :" + str(y)
```

Output:

```
Value of e :2.71828182846
Fast Fourier Transform of y :[ 7.5+0.j  -2. -0.5j  0.5+0.j  -2. +0.5j]
```

Matplotlib Library:

With the enhanced capabilities of Python using NumPy and SciPy. Matplotlib is one of the alternatives of MATLAB software for representation of data and its analysis. With open-source nature Python, these libraries are well used among data scientist and researcher.

You can use Matplotlib for plotting 2-dimensional and 3-dimensional data. It also includes error charts, histogram and bar charts in just a few lines of codes. It makes hard and complex data analysis very easy.

85

Exercise

1. Perform the following mathematical equation:

    a((a + b)/(a-b)) + b + 1

    where a = 10 and b = 5

    Code:

    ```
    a = 10
    b = 5

    c = a*((a+b)/(a-b)) + b + 1

    print "Output Value is : %d" %c
    ```

    Output:

    ```
    Output Value is : 36
    ```

2. Take an input array from the user and find its Fast-Fourier transformation.

    Code:

```
import scipy

# input from user
print "Enter an 1-d array :"
inputArray = [int(x) for x in raw_input().split()]

# performing fase-fourier transform on input
output = scipy.fft(inputArray)

# displaying output
print "Fast-Fourier Transform is :" + str(output)
```

Output:

```
Enter an 1-d array :
1 2 1 4 1 5
Fast-Fourier Transform is :[14. +0.00000000e+00j -0.5+2.59807621e+00j  0.5+2.598
07621e+00j
 -8. +5.77315973e-15j  0.5-2.59807621e+00j -0.5-2.59807621e+00j]
```

3. Plot the sine wave using Python program.

Code:

```
"""
Plotting Sine wave
"""
import numpy as np
import matplotlib.pyplot as plot

# range of sine wave
time = np.arange(0, 10, 0.1)

# finding amplitude of sine wave
amp = np.sine(time)

# plotting the sine wave
plot.plot(time, amp)
plot.show()
```

Output:

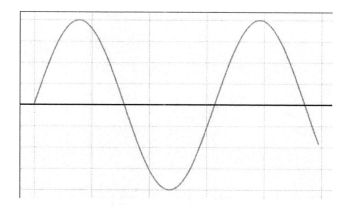

Chapter 7

Data types

In Python, data takes the objects of different types of form – they are either built-in objects provided by the Python language or created by the programmer using Python classes or external language tools. Objects are just pieces of memory used for storing values and set operations on that variable.

Importance of Built-in Types:

In the lower-level language such as C and C++, most of programmer's effort goes into implementing objects to represent the component in the application domain. Being a good programmer, you need to manage memory allocation, memory structure, implement search, and access routine. These chores are very tedious and always distract you from your programming goal.

In the Python language, most of the work goes away as you don't need to do object implementation before you start solving problems. It is always best way to use built-in object instead of implementing your own object.

- Easy to write a program with the help of Built-in Object: Built-in object gives you a collection of lists and dictionaries for free, which is very helpful while working on any task.

- For the complex problem, you need to write your own object with the Python classes and C language interfaces, but it is easier to use built-in types such as list and dictionaries.

- Built-in objects are more efficient than custom data structure because that is already optimized similarly to all data structure algorithms, which is used in C programming language.

To some readers, object types are more powerful while programming. Especially Lists and Dictionary are the more powerful data types, which are very useful in collections and searching in lower-level programming language. Lists provide an ordered collection of objects while dictionary stores object by keys. Lists and dictionary are nested in nature and can grow and shrink according to the demand and also capable to containing the object of any type.

Built-in Objects:

Object Type	Examples
Number	146,2.75,3+4j
String	'python', "programming"
Lists	[1,[4,'six'],6.8]
Dictionaries	{'python': 'programming'}, dict(day=10)
Tuples	(1,'python','U')
Sets	Set('xyz')
Files	Open('egg.txt')
Program unit types	Function, modules, and classes
Implementation relates types	Complied code, stack tracebacks

Other core types	Boolean, Types

Numbers:

Python object also includes the numbers and it contains integer, floating-point numbers, complex numbers, decimal, rational numbers. It supports mathematical operation. For example, plus sign (+) is used for addition, star (*) is used for multiplication, and two stars (**) are sued for exponentiation operation.

Code:

```
>>> 146 + 485
631
>>> 1.3 * 9
11.700000000000001
>>> 2*16
32
>>> 
```

Besides the expression, you can also use numeric modules, which are shipped with Python-modules. They are just Python packages that you can import and add to your program for ease.

Code:

```
>>> import math
>>> math.sqrt(25)
5.0
>>> import random
>>> random.choice([1,2,3,4,5,6])
1
>>>
```

Strings:

Strings are usually used to represent both textual and arbitrary information. String supports an operation that includes positional ordering among items. For example, if you want to calculate the length of a string which is inside quotes, you can use built-in len function and calculate its length.

```
>>> Var = 'Python'
>>> len(Var)
6
>>> Var[2]
't'
>>>
```

In Python, indexes are coded as offset and it start from 0: the first item which is at first place is index 0, second is index 1, and so on. In Python, you can also use of index backward from the endpoint. Positive indexes are counted from the left-hand side and negative numbers count from the right-hand side.

In simple positional indexing, sequences also support slicing in, which you can extract entire section from the string in a single step.

```
>>> Var = 'Python'
>>> len(Var)
6
>>> Var[-1]
'n'
>>> Var[-2]
'o'
>>> Var
'Python'
>>> Var[1:3]
'yt'
>>> █
```

We have seen in previous examples of changing an original string with some operation. We were just generating a new string with every operation because strings are immutable in Python. We can't change a string after they are created. For example, we can't change a string by assigning it to one particular position, but we can create a new string and assign it to the same variable because Python always cleans up an old object.

```
>>> Var = 'Python'
>>> len(Var)
6
>>> Var[-1]
'n'
>>> Var[-2]
'o'
>>> Var
'Python'
>>> Var[1:3]
'yt'
>>> Var[0] = 'z'
Traceback (most recent call last):
  File "<stdin>", line 1, in <module>
TypeError: 'str' object does not support item assignment
>>> Var = 'z' + Var[1:]
>>> Var
'zython'
>>>
```

But, you have one method by which you can change a specific word in the string, but that method is text-based. You can change text-based data if you expand it into individual characters and join it back together or use newer bytearray type available in Python's newer version.

```
>>> Var = 'python'
>>> Var1 = list(Var)
>>> Var1
['p', 'y', 't', 'h', 'o', 'n']
>>> Var1[1] = 'z'
>>> ''.join(Var1)
'pzthon'
```

Every string operation which we have used untill now is like a sequence operation and it can also be used in other Python sequences such as lists and tuples.

String find operation is basic method to search particular substring in string, and string replace method performs replacement of substring in a string. For example,

```
>>> Var = 'python'
>>> Var.find('yt')
1
>>> Var
'python'
>>> Var.replace('py','ze')
'zethon'
```

Here, despite the name of datatype string, we are creating a new string. We are not changing an old string because strings are immutable.

So far, we were understanding the specific operations on the string. But the Python language provides a variety of methods to perform on a string. Some special characters are represented with a backslash. For example, \n is used for end of the line and \t is used for the tab.

You can represent multiple string literals enclosed in triple quotes. Triple quotes are used when you want to concatenate more than one string. For example,

>>>Var = """python""programming"""""

Python language comes with full Unicode support, which is required for processing text in international characters like Japanese, Chinese, or other characters which are outside of the ASCII set. You can see non ASCII character sets in web pages, emails, GUIs, or elsewhere. Python has built-in support for Unicode character, but the form varies per Python line.

One point is worth remembering is that Python support pattern-based text processing. Text pattern matching is an advanced tool for Python for beginners, but the readers who have knowledge of other scripting languages knows the importance of pattern matching. This module is used for searching, splitting, and replacement. For example,

Code:

```
>>> import re
>>> match = re.match('Hello[ \t]*(.*)world', 'Hello   Python world')
>>> match.group(1)
'Python '
>>>
```

The above example searches for the word "Hello" followed by zero or more tabs or spaces, then any character is saved as a match group ending "world". If you find such a substring that matches partial patterns enclosed in parentheses, they are the available group.

Till now, we have studied about numbers and strings in data-types. We are going to study about List, tuple, and dictionary in the upcoming chapter in detail.

Exercise

1. What is a Datatype?

    Answer: The type of data in programming that specifies, what type of value a variable can store such as integer, boolean, string, etcetera.

2. Name fundamental data types present in the Python language.

    Answer:

    - Numbers
    - Boolean
    - String
    - Tuples
    - Lists
    - Dictionary

Chapter 8

Lists and Tuples

Till now, we have learned about different data types and discussed in-details of numbers and strings, which are only two data types in the Python language. Now, we need to understand some more such as Lists and Tuples in detail.

It is really comfortable to deal with the structured format data as the data is set in a specific manner. Python provides data types named "lists" and "Tuples", which is used to organize data in a structured manner. "Lists" and "Tuples" are most popular built-in sequence of the Python language.

Lists:

The Lists are a more flexible ordered collection data type in Python. Unlike strings, lists can contain all type of data such as numbers, strings, and even other lists, too. Lists are mutable in nature so you can change it while assigning and slices.

Properties of Lists:

- Collection of arbitrary objects:
  Lists are the entity where you can collect other objects and treat them as an ordered group. Lists maintain items in left to right positional ordering.

- Accessed by offset:

  In order to access a component, you can fetch any component by indexing the lists. You can fetch it even when it is out of the list. The indexing on object's offset is required for fetching. You can do slicing and concatenation on items because items are set by their position.

- Variable length, nesting:
  Unlike string, lists can grow and shrink according to the need of the program. In addition to that, lists can contain all kinds of objects such as numbers, strings, and another list.

- Mutable:

     You can change lists at any place and it
     responds to all operations, which are performed
     on lists like slicing, indexing, and concatenation.
     It will give result in new lists instead of the new
     string even if you are changing in a string.

- Object reference:

     Python lists contain zero or more than zero
     references to the other objects. Whenever you
     use reference, Python always prefers a reference
     to an object. For example, you are assigning an
     object to the data structure component and
     variable name, then Python will store a
     reference to the same object name. It will not
     store the reference to the copy of that object.

Create Lists:

When you want to build a list, you just need to write the
number of expressions in square bracket.

Syntax:

     lst_1 = [ ]

$$lst\_2 = [expression1, expression2, \ldots\ldots\ldots ,$$

expression N]

For example:

```
list1 = ['script', 'python', 'perl'];
list2 = [1983, 2011];
list3 = [2,4,6, "s", "v", "d"]];
```

Access value in Lists:

Lists len(L) always returns the number of items which is present in the list and L[i] represents the items which is at index i and L[i:j] returns a new list which contains objects between "I' and "j".

Code:

```
list1 = ['script', 'python', 'perl'];
list2 = [1983, 2011];
list3 = [2,4,6, "s", "v", "d"];

print ("list1[0]", list1[0])
print ("list3[2:4]", list3[2:4])
```

Output:

```
('list1[0]', 'script')
('list3[2:4]', [6, 's'])
```

Update Lists:

You can add and update single and multiple elements in a list at a time.

Code:

```
list1 = ['script', 'python', 'perl'];

print ("Third value in list is: ")
print (list1[2])

list1[2] = 'programming language'

print ("Updated value in the list is: ")
print(list1[2])
```

Output:

```
Third value in list is:
perl
Updated value in the list is:
programming language
```

Delete elements from Lists:

"del" statement is used for deleting an element from the list.

Syntax:

Del list_name[index_val];

Lists support many operations similar to string. Lists also respond to arithmetic operations same as string, but it will give the result as a new list. For example, + operator will accept the same sort of sequence on both sides. If it is not the same sequence, then it will give type error while compilation.

Code:

```
list1 = ['script', 'python', 1983, 2011];

print list1;
del list1[2];
print "After deleting value at index 2 : "
print list1;
```

Output:

```
['script', 'python', 1983, 2011]
After deleting value at index 2 :
['script', 'python', 2011]
```

If you want to concatenate string and lists, then you need to convert the lists to string to vice-versa.

Code:

```
>>> str([1,2]) + "83"
'[1, 2]83'
>>> [1,2] + list("83")
[1, 2, '8', '3']
>>>
```

If you want to check all sequence operation you have performed in the string, you will see that lists are responding to all sequence operation.

Code:

```
>>> l = ['script', 'python', 'perl']
>>> l[2]
'perl'
>>> l[-2]
'python'
>>> l[1:]
['python', 'perl']
```

Indexing and Slicing:

In lists, indexing and slicing work the same as the string because the list is also a sequence. The result of indexing depends on the type of object, which is specified by the programmer at the offset, while slicing always give a new list.

Code:

```
>>> l = ['script', 'python', 'perl']
>>> l[1] = 'java'
>>> l
['script', 'java', 'perl']
>>> l[0:2] = ['program', 'language']
>>> l
['program', 'language', 'perl']
```

Change place in the Lists:

Lists always support the operation which changes the place of the object. Python deals with the object references. The creation of new object and change in place always matters while dealing with a reference because it can impact more than one reference.

While using list, you can change its content by assigning it to the offset or slice.

Code:

```
>>> l = ['script', 'python', 'perl']
>>> l.append('java')
>>> l
['script', 'python', 'perl', 'java']
>>> l.sort()
>>> l
['java', 'perl', 'python', 'script']
```

Both index and slice assignment modify the subject list while dealing with in-place. It will not generate a new lists object. Python list support type-specific method calls. Methods are the function, which is associated with and act upon particular objects. It provides type-specific tools which are generally available for lists.

Tuple:

In the Python language, a tuple is a data type which constructs simple group of objects. You cannot change tuples in place and they are written as a series of items in parentheses, not square brackets.

Properties:

- **An ordered collection of arbitrary object:**

    Tuples maintain left to right order when storing any content. It is a collection of objects which are in a positional order. Tuples can embed all kinds of objects.

- **Access by Offset:**

    You can access items by offset and it supports all operations, which are offset-based such as indexing and slicing.

- **Immutable:**

    Like string, tuples are also immutable. It supports many of the same operations like string and lists. It will not support any in-place change operation, which is applied to the lists.

- **Fixed-length and Nestable:**

You cannot change the size of a tuple without masking a copy because of its immutable property. Tuples can hold any type of object including lists, dictionary, etc. It also supports arbitrary nesting.

- **Object references:**

    Tuple storage access point to other objects and the index tuples are relatively fast.

Create Tuple:

You can create a tuple by comma separated values.

For example,

Tup1 = ('python', 'programming');

Tup2 = (1, 2, 3, 4, 5);

Access Values in Tuples:

You can access the value by using square brackets for slicing along with an index to obtain the value.

Code:

```
tup1 = ('script', 'python', 'perl');
tup2 = (1983, 2011);
tup3 = (2,4,6,8,10,12,14,16);
print ("tup1[0]", tup1[0])
print ("tup3[2:4]", tup3[2:4])
```

Output:

```
('tup1[0]', 'script')
('tup3[2:4]', (6, 8))
```

Updating Tuples:

Tuples are immutable in nature, so you cannot change or update the value of tuples. But you can create a new tuple from an existing tuple and make changes in the new tuple.

Code:

```
tup1 = (1, 2, 3);
tup2 = ('abc', 'def');
tup3 = tup1 + tup2
print (tup3)
```

Output:

```
(1, 2, 3, 'abc', 'def')
```

Delete Tuple:

You can delete tuple by using "del" statement.

Code:

```
tup1 = (1, 2, 3);
tup2 = ('abc', 'def');
tup3 = tup1 + tup2

del tup3;
print (tup3)
```

Output:

```
Traceback (most recent call last):
  File "edit_tuple.py", line 6, in <module>
    print (tup3)
NameError: name 'tup3' is not defined
```

Basic Tuple Operation:

You can use an arithmetic operation like + and * in the tuple. It also supports concatenation and repetition similar to the string and it will give result in a new tuple.

Expression	Result	Description
Len((0, 1, 2, 3, 4))	5	Length
(1, 2, 3) + (4, 5 ,6)	(1, 2, 3, 4, 5, 6)	Concatenation
('Python',)*2	('Python', ' Python)	Repetition
4 in (0, 1, 2)	False	Membership

Indexing and Slicing:

You can operate indexing and slicing similar to string because of its ordered set of the element.

Var = ('python', 'python', 'python language')

Expression	Result
Var[3]	'python language'
Var[-3]	'python'
Var[1:]	['python', 'python language']

If you want to compare elements of two tuples, then you can use 'cmp'.

Syntax:

Cmp(tuple_1, tuple_2)

Description:

tuple_1 = first tuple to be compared.

tuple_2 = second tuple to be compared.

If you are comparing elements of the same type, it will give you a direct result, but if you are comparing different types of elements, then you need to cross-check whether it is a number or not. If it is a number, then first perform numeric coercion and then compare them. If they are a string, then it will sorted alphabetically.

Code:

```
tup1 ,tup2 = (123, 'abc'), (456, 'xyz')
print cmp(tup1, tup2);
print cmp(tup2, tup1);
tup3 = tup2 + (789,);
print cmp(tup2, tup3)
```

Output:

```
-1
1
-1
```

If you want to find the length of tuple, then you can use "len()". It will return the number of element in the tuple.

Syntax:

len(tuple)

Description:

Tuple = tuple in which you need to count numbers of elements.

Code:

```
tup1, tup2 = (123, 'abc', 'pqrs'),(456, 'xyz')
print "first tuple length : ", len(tup1);
print "Second tuple length: ", len(tup2);
```

Output:

```
first tuple length :  3
Second tuple length:  2
```

Exercise

1. Explain Lists using Python program.

Answer: The lists are the most flexible ordered collection data type in Python. Unlike strings, lists contain all type of data such as numbers, strings, and even other lists, too. Lists are mutable in nature, so you can change it while assigning and slices.

Code:

```
list1 = ['script', 'python', 'perl'];
list2 = [1983, 2011];
list3 = [2,4,6, "s", "v", "d"];
```

2. Explain Tuples using Python program.

Answer: In the Python language, a tuple is a data type which constructs simple group of objects. You cannot change tuples in place and they are written as a series of items in parentheses, not square brackets.

Code:

```
tup1 = ('script', 'python', 'perl');
tup2 = (1983, 2011);
tup3 = (2,4,6,8,10,12,14,16);
print ("tup1[0]", tup1[0])
print ("tup3[2:4]", tup3[2:4])
```

Chapter 9

Dictionaries

After string, list, tuple, and numbers, dictionaries is a popular used data type in the Python programming language. It is the last data type to understand in this material. Dictionaries are completely different from other data types. They are not in sequence at all, but still, it is known as mapping.

Mapping is also considered as a collection of other objects, but it stores them as keys instead of their position as the tuple. Mapping doesn't follow any left to right order like tuple; it directly maps keys to associated values.

Properties:

- **Access by keys:** Dictionaries associate a key, so you can fetch an item using the keys from the dictionary. Indexing operation is the same as the list to get component in a dictionary, but the difference between

116

them is it takes the form of the keys and does not use a relative offset.

- **Unordered collection of object:** Items stored in dictionaries are not in order, unlike a list. Keys provide a location of items in a dictionary, but it provides the only symbolic location. It does not provide a physical location, too.

- **Variable length and nesting:** Dictionaries can contain any type of objects and it supports nesting to any depth, too. There can be only one key per key value, but if necessary, the value can be a collection of multiple objects, and a given value can be stored under any number of keys. Dictionaries can grow and shrink without new copies.

- **Mutable:** Dictionaries can be modified by assigning value to indexes, but it does not support sequence operation unlike string and lists because dictionaries are an unordered collection.

- **Object references:** Dictionaries are an unordered table of object references that support access by keys. It is implemented similarly to a hash table, which starts small and grows as per the need. Python uses a optimization hash table algorithm to find the keys — it helps to retrieve data quickly. Like lists, dictionaries also store object references.

Dictionaries Usage:

You can use an arbitrary object such as the standard object or user-defined object in dictionary values. Its values don't have any restrictions on using Python objects, but you cannot use all Python objects with the keys.

There are some points you need to remember about dictionary keys:

- You cannot do more than one entry per key. It means you cannot use a duplicate key. If duplicate keys are encountered during assignment, it takes the last assignment into consideration

- Key should be immutable, which means you can use string, tuples, etc. as dictionary keys, but you cannot use 'key'.

Access Value in Dictionary:

If you want to access elements in the dictionary, you can use the square bracket with the key.

Code:

```
dict = {'Name' : 'Smith', 'Age' : 25}
print (dict['Name'])
print (dict['Age'])
```

Output:

```
Smith
25
```

If you are trying to access elements which are not present in the dictionary, then it will show you an error.

Code:

```
dict = {'Name' : 'Smith', 'Age' : 25, 'Class' : 'Seven'};
print "dict['Mark']: ", dict['Mark'];
```

Output:

```
dict['Mark']:
Traceback (most recent call last):
  File "access_dict.py", line 2, in <module>
    print "dict['Mark']: ", dict['Mark'];
KeyError: 'Mark'
```

Update Dictionary:

You can update a dictionary by adding a new entry, or you can modify or delete an existing entry.

Code:

```
dict = {'Name': 'Smith', 'Age': 10, 'Class': 'Seven'};
dict['Age'] = 14; # update existing entry
dict['School'] = "DPS School"; # Add new entry
print "dict['Age']: ", dict['Age'];
print "dict['School']: ", dict['School'];
```

Output:

```
dict['Age']:  14
dict['School']:  DPS School
```

Delete Dictionary Element:

Dictionary gives you an option of deleting individual elements in the dictionary or deleting entire content, which is present in the dictionary, or you can delete the entire dictionary in a single operation.

You can use "del" statement to remove the entire dictionary.

Code:

```
dict = {'Name': 'Smith', 'Age': 10, 'Class': 'Seven'};
del dict['Name']; # remove entry with key 'Name'
dict.clear(); # remove all entries in dict
del dict ; # delete entire dictionary
print "dict['Age']: ", dict['Age'];
print "dict['School']: ", dict['School'];
```

Output:

```
dict['Age']:
Traceback (most recent call last):
  File "delete_dict.py", line 5, in <module>
    print "dict['Age']: ", dict['Age'];
TypeError: 'type' object has no attribute ' getitem '
```

Dictionary Functions:

1. cmp(dictionary1, dictionary2)

2. len(dictionary)

3. str(dictionary)

4. type(variable)

cmp(dictionary1,dictionary2):

This method is used to compare elements of both dictionaries. It compares both dictionaries based on key and values.

Syntax:

cmp(dictionary1, dictionary2)

Parameters:

121

Dictionary1 = First dictionary to be compared with dictionary2.

Dictionary2 = Second dictionary to be compared with dictionary1.

Code:

```
dict1 = {'Name': 'Zara', 'Age': 7};
dict2 = {'Name': 'Smith', 'Age': 27};
dict3 = {'Name': 'Mark', 'Age': 25};
dict4 = {'Name': 'Adam', 'Age': 10};
print "Return Value : %d" % cmp (dict1, dict2)
print "Return Value : %d" % cmp (dict2, dict3)
print "Return Value : %d" % cmp (dict1, dict4)
```

Output:

```
Return Value : -1
Return Value : 1
Return Value : -1
```

It will return 0 if both dictionaries are equal (dict1 = dict2) in comparison.

If dictionary1 is greater than dictionary2 (dict1>dict2) then it will return 1.

If dictionary2 is greater than dictionary1 (dict2>dict1) then it will return -1.

len(dictionary):

122

This method gives the length of the dictionary. It counts the number of items and gives the result as a length of the dictionary.

Syntax:

len(dictionary)

Parameters:

Dictionary: Dictionary's length you need to calculate.

Code:

```
dict = {'Name': 'Smith', 'Age': 10};
print "Length : %d" % len (dict)
```

Output:

```
Length : 2
```

str(dictionary):

This method is used to produce a printable string which can represent the dictionary.

Syntax:

str(dictionary)

Parameters:

Dictionary: It is a dictionary.

It will return a string representation.

Code:

```
dict = {'Name': 'Smith', 'Age': 10};
print "Equivalent String : %s" % str (dict)
```

Output:

```
Equivalent String : {'Age': 10, 'Name': 'Smith'}
```

type(dictionary):

This method is used to return the type of variable that you are passing. If passing variable is dictionary then its return type is of dictionary data type.

Syntax:

type(dictionary)

Parameters:

Dictionary: It is a dictionary.

It returns the type of variable that you are passing to the dictionary.

Code:

```
dict = {'Name': 'Smith', 'Age': 10};
print "Variable Type : %s" %type (dict)
```

Output:

```
Variable Type : <type 'dict'>
```

Sorting keys:

Dictionaries are not in sequence, they don't maintain any left to right order, so when you are printing it, it may come with the different order. If you want all of the dictionary items in proper order, than you can use the dictionary key method to get the key list, sort them by sort method, then iterate through the results in Python for loops. The sorted call returns the result and sorts the various object types sorted in the case dictionary key automatically.

Exercise

1. What is Mapping?

Answer: Mapping is considered a collection of other objects, but it stores them with keys instead of their position. Mapping doesn't follow any left to right order like tuple, it directly maps keys to associated values.

2. Why we need Dictionary?

Answer: You can use an arbitrary object such as the standard object or user-defined object in dictionary values. Its values don't have any restrictions on using Python objects. But, you cannot use all Python objects with the keys.

There are some points which you need to remember about dictionary keys:

- You cannot do more than one entry per key. It means you cannot use duplicate key. If duplicate keys have encountered during assignment, then it takes last assignment into consideration

- Key should be immutable, which means you can use string, tuples, etc. as dictionary keys, but you cannot use 'key'.

Chapter 10

Control Statements

Introduction:

The Python language execution is sequential in nature, but in some cases, you need to change your program's execution sequence based on the problem requirement. Sometimes, you even need to check some conditions, and based on the condition fulfilment, statements need to be executed. To fulfil this requirement, Python provides features like conditional execution, iterative execution, and jumps in the program. They specify the transfer of control from one line to another.

For the conditional execution of statements, Python provides:

1. If-else

2. Switch-case

   For the iterative execution of the code, Python provides:

1. While loop

2. For loop

3. Nested loop

   For jumps in the program, Python has rich features of break and continue. Let's discuss all there feature in detail:

If-else :

This is the most common and powerful feature to implement condition execution of the statement in Python. It is bidirectional in nature. The syntax is as follows:

If expression:

   Statement1

Else:

   Statement2

In the above syntax, Python interpreter evaluates the expression, also called if condition. If the expression results in true (non zero) then statement1 executes. Otherwise, statement2 execution takes place. The following flowchart is suitable for the better understanding of its bidirectional nature:

Flowchart

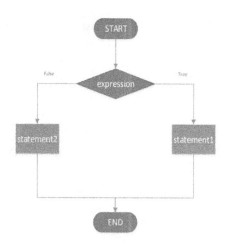

Code

```
"""
Program to check Even and Odd number
"""
num = int(raw_input("Enter a Number :"))
if (num%2==0):
        print "Number is Even"
else:
        print "Number is Odd"
```

Output

```
Enter a Number :5
Number is Odd
```

It is also possible to keep multiple statements with if-else to executes. It just requires putting same indentation space. Block of statements with the same indentation is also called compound statement. The syntax with compound statements is as follows:

If expression:

      Statement1

      Statement2

Else:

      Statement3

      Statement4

FlowChart

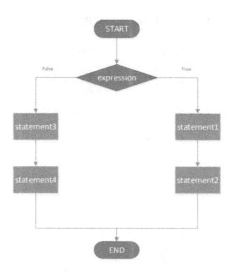

Code

```
"""
Program to test Even and Odd number and display it
"""
num = int(raw_input("Enter a Number :"))
if (num%2 == 0):
        print "Entered number is " + str(num)
        print "Number is Even"
else:
        print "Entered number is " + str(num)
        print "Number is Odd"
```

Output

```
Enter a Number :45
Entered number is 45
Number is Odd
```

Else part of the syntax is not compulsory. You can skip it, according to the need. The syntax and flowchart are as following:

If expression

    statement1

Flowchart3

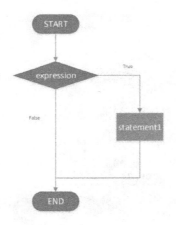

Code

```
o rr rr
Program to test even number
rr rr rr
num = int(raw_input("Enter a Number :"))
if (num%2 == 0):
        print "Entered number is " + str(num)
        print "Number is Even"
```

Output

```
Enter a Number :78
Entered number is 78
Number is Even
```

Nested if-else:

The Python language also allows the nesting of if-else where one if-else statement can be used inside the body of other if-else as following:

If expression1:

    If expression2:

        Statement1

    Else

        Statement2

Else

    If expression3:

        Statement3

    Else:

        Statement4

Flowchart

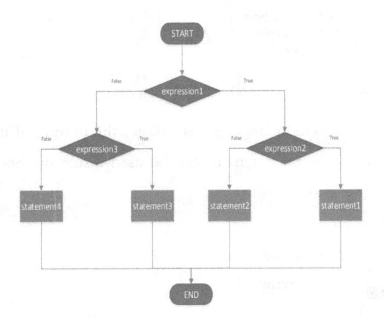

Code

```
"""
Program to find the input range of number
"""
num = int(raw_input("Enter a Number(between 0 to 200):"))
if (num < 100):
        if (num > 50):
                print "Entered number is between 50 and 100"
        else:
                print "Entered number is between 0 and 50"
else:
        if (num > 150):
                print "Entered number is between 150 and 200"
        else:
                print "Entered number is between 100 and 150"
```

Output

```
Enter a Number(between 0 to 200):100
Entered number is between 100 and 150
```

Else-if Ladder:

The else-if ladder is one type of multi-way decision-making statement in Python. There is an if-else statement for every else part of if statement and the syntax for the same is as follows:

If expresion1:

    Statement1

Elif expression2:

    Statement2

Elif expression3:

    Statement3

Else:

    Statement4

In the else-if ladder, Python interpreter evaluates every if condition sequentially one-by-one, and when it resolves into true, it executes the corresponding statement and then controls comes out without checking remaining condition.

Flowchart

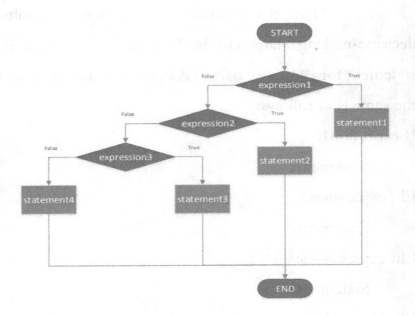

Code

```
"""
Program to test number range
"""
num = int(raw_input("Enter a Number(between 0 to 100):"))
if (num < 25):
        print "Number is between 0 to 25"
elif (num < 50):
        print "Number is between 25 to 50"
elif (num < 75):
        print "Number is between 50 to 75"
else:
        print "Number is between 75 to 100"
```

Output

```
Enter a Number(between 0 to 100):50
Number is between 50 to 75
```

Loops:

137

In any programming language, loops are used when we want to execute a part of program multiple times. It is always easy to optimize the program using Loops. For example, if you want to print a string "Welcome to Python" ten times on the output string, instead of writing print statement ten times, you can use one of the loops (while or for) to implement it. Every Loop in the Python language requires a counter variable, condition check, and increment or decrement operation.

Counter variable keeps track of the number of times the loop has executed. Increment and decrement operation is implemented on the counter variable, and condition check is required for termination of the loop.

Each loop has its own requirement and significance during programming. Let's understand them in detail:

While Loop:

The syntax of while loop is as following:

While expression:
  Statement1
  Statement2

In the above syntax, the expression is evaluated by the interpreter first, and if it resolves into true, then the body of the while loop (Compound Statements) executes. Otherwise, it comes out of the loop. After the execution of the body again, it evaluates the expression and executes the body. The body of loop will execute until the expression in the results into false. This process can be better understood from the below flow chart.

Flowchart

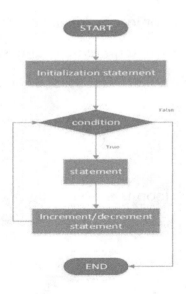

In the programming, you can use the following type of convention for more productive code.

Initialization statement

While condition:

    Statement

    Increment/decrement statement

You will get a clear idea for above convention with the following programming challenge.

Code

```
"""
Program to print 1 to 10 using while-loop
"""
i = 1
while (i <= 10):
        print i
        i = i + 1
```

Output:

```
1
2
3
4
5
6
7
8
9
10
```

For Loop:

The for loop is frequently used out of all the loops because of its easy syntax, which is as follows:

For counterVar in sequence:
 Statements

The syntax comprises of counterVar variable and a sequence. The sequence could be either list, tuple, string, or any collection of data. If you are dealing with data sequencing in Python, for loop is definitely a feasible choice.

During the execution of for loop, the first element in the sequence is assigned to the counterVar and statements of the loop body are executed, then the next element is assigned to the couterVar and the statements are executed in a loop until all the elements of the sequence are exhausted. The sequence in the loop could be any list, string, or collection of data elements.

Flowchart

When you need to iterate through the sequence, there are two ways you can iterate using for loop. Let's understand them in brief:

1. Iterating using Sequence expression:

    In this type of for loop, the programmer uses the following syntax to iterate in for loop.

    For element in Sequence:

           Statements

Code

```
"""
Program to print list elements using for-loop
"""
list = ["python","programming","is","fun"]

for list_element in list:
        print list_element
```

Output

```
python
programming
is
fun
```

2. Iterating using Sequence Index:

In this type of for loop, the programmer uses the following syntax to iterate in for loop.

For index in range(len(Sequence)):

    Statements

Code

```
"""
Program to print list elements using for-loop
"""
list = ["python","programming","is","fun"]

for index in range(len(list)):
        print list[index]
```

Output

```
python
programming
is
fun
```

Nesting of loops is also possible by using one loop inside the body of another loop. Application of nested loops can be in the array of sequence and for handling huge data.

Infinite Loop:

The loops that execute its body infinite times are known as the infinite loop. You can implement this type of loop deliberately or by mistake, which puts your program running into continuously. To implement infinite loop, you can use the following approach:

While True:

Statement

The termination of an infinite loop can be controlled by using break and goto statement inside the body of the loop. These statements are explained in the further topics of this chapter.

Continue and Break Statement:

Continue and break statements are very useful statements and used frequently with loops. The syntax for continue is simple:

Continue

Continue statement is used for skipping execution of the loop statements inside the loop body and transferring control to the beginning of the next loop iteration. It is used with the if condition generally. Let's understand its use case with a programming challenge

Code

```
"""
Program to skip numbers using 6 to 10 using continue statement
"""
i = 0
while i<10:
    i = i + 1
    if i == 5:
        continue
    print i
```

Output

```
1
2
3
4
6
7
8
9
10
```

The break statement is similar to the continue, but when it is used inside the loop, it terminates the loop and control is transferred to the next statement after the loop. Let's understand it with following program.

Code

```
"""
Program to stop while-loop using break statement
"""
i = 0
while (i<10):
        i = i + 1
        if (i > 5):
                break
        print i
```

Output

```
1
2
3
4
5
```

Exercise

1. What is the importance of loops in programming?

    Answer: Defining a loop in your code allows the computer to repeatedly perform certain tasks. Depending on the task to be performed, the loop needs to be defined in the computer program for a variety of reasons. The computer programming language needs to be looped so that the code executes actions as many times as needed.

2. Name different types of available loops in Python.

    Answer:
    - For loop
    - While loop
    - Infinite loop using for and while loop

Chapter 11

Functions and Modules

Introduction:

Throughout the previous chapters, we have discussed the different features of Python interpreter that will help you to create your Python program. It's time to move to the design approaches for your programs and without an understanding of the functions and modules, it would be impossible to create a properly designed program. Functions and Modules give you the freedom to cut your program into small parts and implement it with an easy-to-design philosophy.

Functions and its Uses:

In simple words, a function is a collective group of Python statements. The ideology behind the use of functions is to reuse the code. Whenever you come across a situation where you want to execute a group of statements more than once, then you need to create a function. It is a programming practice to write a function and call it with its name every time. You can also perceive functions as the independently running programming section, that you can use multiple times.

Functions are like devices that have the capability of taking input parameters and provide output. Output of the function can be either a data or operation on the parameter passed in it.

Before we dig deep into the syntax and programming with functions, let's understand a bigger picture for the use case of functions. Functions are generally giving a structure to your Python program. Sometimes they are also called procedures and sub-routines in other programming languages. Primarily, there are following philosophy for the use of functions in any python program:

1. Maximum Code-reuse and Minimum redundant programming:
   It is similar to any other programming language. Functions are the easiest way to package your Python logic, you just need to write your code logic once in the

function body, and later you can use it multiple times in your program. It also minimizes your redundant statements.

2. Well-structured programming:

The function gives you a tool to divide your big programming task into multiple well-defined procedures and allow you have a well-structured program for the same. Let's consider a programming scenario where you want to calculate average salary of the employee in any organization. You can divide the task into procedures likes taking the input of the employee data, calculating an average, and displaying the average value. The function can be written for each of the procedures and call them to have the well-structured program.

Function Syntax:

In Python programming, the general syntax of writing function is as follows:

```
def functionName( arg1, arg2 …. argN):
    Statements
    Return val
```

def is considered as the header of the function, which generates a function object and assigns a function name to it. In the brackets, the function multiple input parameters are represented with arg1, arg2 … argN. These arguments are optional when the function does not take any input parameter then brackets are kept empty. After the colon, function bodies with multiple statements is written where functional logic is implemented. The return statement returns val value to the caller in the program. It can appear anywhere inside the function body and usually is present at the end of the function. If val is not specified, then function returns None as the return value. Both the val and return statement are optional.

Let's get into the Python programming to get more use out of case of functions and its implementation:

Code

```
"""
Program to add two numbers using a function
"""
def main():
        num1 = 10
        num2 = 20
        num3 = add( num1, num2)
        print "Addition is :" + str(num3)

def add( a, b):
        c = a + b
        return c

if __name__ == "__main__":
        main()
```

Output

```
Addition is :30
```

Code

```
"""
Program to test even odd using function
"""
def main():
        input_num = int(raw_input("Enter a Number :"))
        evenOdd(input_num)

def evenOdd(num):
    if (num%2 == 0):
            print "Number is Even"
    else:
            print "Number is Odd"
    return

if __name__ == "__main__":
        main()
```

Output

```
Enter a Number :45
Number is Odd
```

Modules and its Uses:

Modules are the top level programs which organize programming units. It contains packages that have Python code, reusable data, and namespaces, which reduces clashing of variables in your Python program. In a simple way, modules can be considered as the program files. And every file which is referred is called as a Module.

Modules are generally processed by using import and from statement. Let's understand about these statements before digging into deep into modules:

1. Import:

    It allows you to load complete module as a whole in your Python program.

2. From:

    It allows you to load specific names from any module in your Python program.

As any particular module is being loaded inside your Python program, it lets you use all the self-contained program codes from the modules. Because of the use of modules inside Python programming, it provides you with a bigger picture with the use of existing modules without any conflicts between attributes and methods.

There are many uses of modules, let's understand them in a brief:

1. Code – reuse:

    When you are loading any of the modules in your Python using import statement, you can use all the methods and functions present in the particular module. After importing, it can be referenced multiple times to reduce the lines of code. Modules always help to visualize a bigger picture of the program. Unless you are using Python interpreter, you can import modules just by using its name.

2. Separate Namespaces:

   As modules are a self-contained program code, being a programmer, their parameters are isolated from your main Python code. It helps you to write your Python code in a well-organized manner, keeping top-level organization in mind.

Whenever you are working with Python programming, you will need to import and link libraries with your main top-level program. Libraries are present inside the module files, which act as a tool to perform programming tasks.

Let's understand the concept of modules and its use with programming examples. There are following files with their Python code:

Def display(text):   #displayModule.py

     Print text

```
Import displayModule                          #
mainScript.py

displayModule.display("Hello, World!!")        # prints
"Hello, World!!"
```

In the above example, "mainScript.py" is a top-level file that contains text in it. The execution of the top-level file occurs in a top to bottom. And "displayModule.py" are modules files containing def statements and assigns function object to the name "display". Inside the function body, print statement is present and displays the passing parameter to the output screen.

The top-level files include an import statement that loads the modules into the main file. After fetching modules, it can be referenced using the attributes of it.

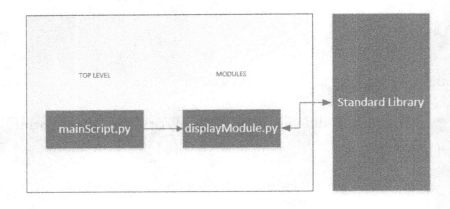

Exercise

1. What is Function and write uses of function in a programming language?

    Answer: In simple words, a function is a collective group of Python statements. The ideology behind the use of functions is to reuse the code. Whenever you come across a situation where you want to execute a group of statements more than once, then you need to create a function. It is a programming practice to write a function and call it every time with its name. You can also perceive functions as the independently running programming section, which you can use multiple times.

    Functions are like devices that have the capability of taking input parameters and provide output. The output of the function can be either a data or operation on the parameter passed in it.

2. What are modules and its uses?

Answer: Modules are the top level programs that organize programming units. It contains packages that have Python code, reusable data, and namespaces which reduces clashing of variables in your Python program. In a simple way, modules can be considered as the program files, and every file, which is referred is called as a Module.

- When you are loading any of the modules in your Python using import statement. You can use all the methods and functions present in the particular module. After importing, it can be referenced multiple times that reduce the lines of code. Modules always help to visualize a bigger picture of the program. Unless you are using Python interpreter, you can import modules just by using its name.

- As modules are self-contained program codes, being a programmer, their parameters are isolated from your main Python code. It helps you to write your Python code in a well-organized manner with top-level organization in mind.

Chapter 12

File Input-Output

Each program is a combination of program statements to perform some task or logic. These logics may or may not require inputs to provide the output, hence inputs that are outputted are part of every program. You need a file to store everything for storage on the computer, which is managed by OS. Although variable provides us a way to store the data while a program is running, we must save it to a file if we want to keep the data after the program has ended.

There are always two parts of a computer system's file, one is a filename and another is an extension of the file. In addition, these files also have two key attributes, which are name and location or path which specify the location of file in the computer. The two parts of the filename are separated by dots (.) or periods.

The built-in open method is used to create a Python file object that provides a connection to the files, which resides on the programmer's machine. After calling an open function, the programmer can transfer the data string to and from an external file residing in the machine.

Print to the screen

You can produce output by using the "print" statement where you can pass expression separated by commas. This function converts the expression which you are passing into a string and writes the result to standard output.

Code:

```
print "python is widely used programming language";
```

Output:

```
python is widely used programming language
```

Read Input:

You can read a line of text from standard input, which will come from the keyboard by using two built-in functions.

- raw_input

- input

- **raw_input function:**

  The raw_input function reads one line from standard input and returns output as string.

Code:

```
str = raw_input("Enter string: ");
print "input is: ", str
```

Output:

```
Enter string: Hello python
input is:  Hello python
```

- **input function:**

  The input function assumes that the input is a valid Python expression and it will return the evaluated result to you.

Code:

```
str = input("Enter string: ");
print "input is: ", str
```

Output:

```
Enter string: [x*5 for x in range(2,10,2)]
input is:  [10, 20, 30, 40]
```

Open and close the file:

From the beginning of this chapter, we understood the function related to input and output from the users. In the continuing discussion, we will have an in-depth understanding of taking inputs from the file and storing the output to it.

Open Function:

You need to open file before you start reading and writing any file. Python has a built-in function that is used to open file i.e. open(). This function will create a file object, which is utilized to call other methods associated with it.

Syntax:

File object = open(file_name[, access_mode][, buffering])

Parameters:

file_name = The file_name is a string value which contains a file name to access.

access_mode = The access mode provides the mode in which the programmer wants to open the file i.e. read, write, append etc.

buffering = If buffer value is 0, that means no buffering. If it is 1, then line buffering is performed while accessing the file. If you specify the buffer value as a greater than 1, then buffer the operation execute with the specified buffer size. If it is negative, the buffer size is system default.

Different Modes:

Modes	Description
R	Open file for read only
r+	Open file for both read and write
rb	Open file for read in binary format
rb+	Open file for both read and write in a binary format
W	Open file for write only
w+	Open file for both read and write
wb	Open file for write in a binary format

wb+	Open file for both read and write in a binary format
A	Open file for appending
a+	Open file for both appending and reading
ab	Open file for appending in binary format
ab+	Open file for both appending and reading in binary format

Close Function:

The close () method of the file object refreshes any unwritten information and closes the object file and the object cannot be written later.

Python closes the file automatically when the file is reassigned to another file.

Syntax:

fileObject.close();

Code:

```
foo = open("python|.txt", "wb")
print "Name of the file: ", foo.name
foo.close()
```

Output:

```
Name of the file:  python.txt
```

Read and Write the file:

Write Function:

You can write any string to an open file by using write () function. It is really important that Python string contains binary data and not just text. It does not add a new line character to the end of the string.

Syntax:

fileObject.write(string);

Code:

```
foo = open("python.txt", "wb")
foo.write( "Python is a widely used programming language.\nYeah its great!!\n");
foo.close()
```

Output:

```
Python is a widely used programming language.
Yeah its great!!
```

The above method will create .text file and writes content in the file, and after execution, it closes the file.

Read Function:

You can read a string from an open file by using read () function.

Syntax:

fileObject.read([count]);

Parameters:

The passing parameter is representing the number of bytes to be read from the open file. This method starts reading from the beginning of the file, and if count is missing, then it tries to read as much as possible, maybe until the file is over.

<u>Code:</u>

```
foo = open("python.txt", "r+")
str = foo.read(10);
print "Read String is : ", str
foo.close()
```

Output:

```
Name of the file:  python.txt
Closed or not :  False
Opening mode :  wb
Softspace flag :  0
happy@happy-300E4C-300E5C-300E7C:~/python$ gedit open.py
happy@happy-300E4C-300E5C-300E7C:~/python$ gedit close.py
happy@happy-300E4C-300E5C-300E7C:~/python$ python close.py
Name of the file:  python.txt
happy@happy-300E4C-300E5C-300E7C:~/python$ gedit close.py
happy@happy-300E4C-300E5C-300E7C:~/python$ gedit write.py
happy@happy-300E4C-300E5C-300E7C:~/python$ python write.py
happy@happy-300E4C-300E5C-300E7C:~/python$ open write.txt
Couldn't get a file descriptor referring to the console
happy@happy-300E4C-300E5C-300E7C:~/python$ gedit python.txt
happy@happy-300E4C-300E5C-300E7C:~/python$ gedit write.py
happy@happy-300E4C-300E5C-300E7C:~/python$ gedit read.py
happy@happy-300E4C-300E5C-300E7C:~/python$ gedit python.txt
happy@happy-300E4C-300E5C-300E7C:~/python$ python read.py
Read String is :  Python is
```

File Position:

If you want to check current position with the file, then you can use *tell()* function. The next read and write will occur after the number of bytes returned from the tell () function from the beginning of the file.

The *seek* (offset [, from]) is used to change the current file position. The offset indicates the number of bytes to move. The *from* is used to specify the reference position from which you want to move the bytes.

If from is set to 0, the beginning of the file is used as a reference position. 1 indicates that the current position is used as a reference position. If it is set to 2, then the end of the file will be treated as a reference position.

Code:

```
foo = open("python.txt", "r+")
str = foo.read(10);
print "Read String is : ", str
position = foo.tell();
print "Current file position : ", position
position = foo.seek(0, 0);
str = foo.read(10);
print "Again read String is : ", str
fool.close()
```

Output:

```
Read String is :  Python is
Current file position :  10
Again read String is :  Python is
```

Rename and Delete File:

Rename Function:

Rename function generally takes two arguments i.e. current filename and new filename.

Syntax:

os.rename(current_filename, new_filename)

Remove Function:

You can delete files by giving the name of the file as an argument in the remove () function.

Syntax:

os.remove(file_name)

Code:

```
import os
# Remove a file python1.txt
os.remove( "python1.txt" )
```

File Flush:

Python automatically flushes the files when it is closed. But if you want to flush the data before closing the file, then you can use flush () function. This method is used to flush the internal buffer.

Syntax:

fileObject.flush();

It does not return any value.

Code:

```
foo = open("python.txt", "wb")
print "Name of the file: ", foo.name
# Here it does nothing, but you can call it with read operation.
foo.flush()
foo.close()
```

Output:

```
Name of the file:  python.txt
```

File next:

The *next* () function is used when the file is used repeatedly or iteratively. It returns the next input line and raises *StopIteration* when end of the line hits.

Using the next () method with other file methods such as *readline* () is not correct. However, using *seek* () to relocate the file to an absolute position refreshes the read-ahead buffer.

Syntax:

fileObject.next();

Next () function will return the next input line.

Code:

```
foo = open("python.txt", "rw+")
print "Name of the file: ", foo.name
# Assuming file has following 3 lines
# This is 1st line
# This is 2nd line
# This is 3rd line
for index in range(3):
   line = foo.next()
   print "Line No %d - %s" % (index, line)
foo.close()
```

Exercise

1. What is the usage of help () and dir () function in Python?

   Answer: The Help () and dir () functions can be accessed from the Python interpreter and used to view merge dumps of built-in functions.

   - Help Function: The help () function is used to display document strings, as well as help with modules, keywords, properties, and more.
   - Dir Function: The dir() is used to display the symbols which is defined.

2. What are negative indexes and where it is used?

   Answer: The sequence in Python is indexed and consists of positive numbers and negative numbers. The positive numbers use '0' as the first index and '1' as the second index, so the process is done.

The negative index begins with '-1', indicating the last index in the sequence, '-2' as the penultimate index, and the sequence going forwards like a positive number.

Chapter 13

Object-oriented Programming

Introduction:

The secondary philosophy behind the development of the Python language was to create an easy-to-code object-oriented programming language that has the capability of less development time with all the advantages of object-oriented. Though using Python's object-oriented way of programming is optional, but it is a good practice over procedural programming.

You can certainly use procedural programming practice with Python, which allows you to develop pretty quickly. In practice, Object-oriented programming requires a lot of pre-planning in the actual development of the solution, hence it is used for the large projects. When the time for the solution development is less, then top-bottom approach in writing Python scripts are a better option. In some situations, if the pre-planning and program modelling strategies are properly formed for larger projects, then development time could be significantly reduced.

If you are not familiar with basics or object-oriented fundamentals, then it is advisable to refer all the basic principles of object-oriented programming. Before getting deep in the object-oriented programming, let's get familiar with various terminologies associated with it:

1. Class:

   The class is a prototype, which is user-defined and specifies a standard set of attributes. These attributes are methods, instance variables, and data variables.

2. Class Variable:

   Class variables are the object or variables which are shared in a particular class. These variables are declared and defined inside the body of a class, but outside of method present in the class. Generally, these types of variables are less commonly used than instance variables.

3. Instance:

A specific object class is called an Instance of that particular class.

4. Instance Variable:

The variables which are declared and defined inside the body of the class method and its scope are only inside the method body.

5. Object:

An object is the basic building block of any object-oriented programming language. It is a particular instance of the data structure that is defined by its class. The object includes methods instance variables and class variables.

6. Method:

The method is a small function or procedure defined inside a class. These are the building blocks of any class that implements certain logic.

7. Inheritance:

Inheritance is one of the popular advantages of using an object-oriented programming language. It is a process in which the characteristics of a class is transferred to the other class. The new class, which is derived from the former class, is also known as the child class.

Now, let's get started with the object-oriented programming in further sections:

Creating a Class:

Classes are the user-defined prototypes with its attributes. To create a class in the Python language. The following syntax is used:

class ClassName:
        "Class Documentation string"
        classAttributes

In the above syntax, the class is a statement that creates a class with class name as className. The next line after the colon is for documentations of class. The documentation string contains all the information about the class in the double inverted comma. The class body has classAttributes and it comprises of class variables, instance variables, and methods.

Example of Class

Let's understand the fundamental of object oriented class with a simple programming example.

Code

```
"""
Program to create Employee Class
"""
class Employee:
        'Base class for Employee'
        employeeCount = 0;

        def __init__(self, name, salary):
                self.name = name
                self.salary = salary
                Employee.employeeCount += 1

        def displayCount(self):
                print "Total Employees are %d" % Employee.employeeCount

        def displayEmployee(self):
                print "Name : ", self.name, ",Salary :", self.salary

# Creating fist object of Employee Class
employee1 = Employee("Alex", 8000)

# Creating second object of Employee Class
employee2 = Employee("Neo", 10000)

# Displaying employee1 and employee2 data
employee1.displayEmployee()
employee2.displayEmployee()

# Displaying totoal number of employee
print "Totol Employee :%d" % Employee.employeeCount
```

Output

```
Name :   Alex ,Salary : 8000
Name :   Neo ,Salary : 10000
Totol Employee :2
```

In the above example, Employee class can have multiple attributes such as Employee name, Employee salary, and their count, hence class allows the programmer to specify

180

the entity with its features. displayCount and displayEmployee are the methods of the Employee class. Inside the Employee class, employeeCount variable is instance variable as its scope is inside the class only.

The method name with __init__ inside the Employee class is called the constructor or initialization method whenever object of Employee class is created, then its attributes are initialized with the specified arguments.

To create an object of the class, it can be called with its name and initialized parameter is passed. In the above program, employee1 and employee2 are two objects of Employee class. To access the attributes of any class, it can be used with className, dot operator, and attribute name. As you can see, to call displayEmployee, method employee1.displayEmployee() is used.

The object-oriented programming philosophy helps in distributing the real time entities as classes and allows the programmer to write modular code and implement it for larger applications.

Exercise

1. What is object oriented programming?

   Answer: OOPS is abbreviated as an object-oriented programming system, in which programs are treated as a collection of objects. Each object is an instance of a class.

2. Explain function overloading?

   Answer: Function overloading is defined as a normal function, but it has the ability to perform different tasks. Through the function input and output types, you can create several methods with the same name.

Chapter 14

Code Optimization

Python is one of the most popular and widely used programming languages for solving programming challenges. There can be many solutions for the particular problem by using different logics, but the effectiveness of any solution is measured in terms of time and memory consumed. If your solution is giving correct output but taking a long time to run, then it is not optimized, it is similar to memory consumption. Your program should be consuming optimum memory. But there is always a trade-off between these two parameters. Because when you try to write high-speed code, then it increases memory consumption of the system and vice versa, but based on the application requirements, one can find a well-optimized solution.

Creating a highly effective solution takes a lot of programming experience and in-depth knowledge of the

Python language. In the further section of this chapter, we have discussed some techniques for finding an optimized solution, they are as following:

- **Use built-in function and library:** Built-in function is really helpful for optimizing any code. The interpreter does not need to execute particular loops so it will give you fast results.

  The packages are platform specific, which means if you are doing string operation, then it is better to use Python packages to optimize your code. For example, use existing module "collection" like "deque" which is an optimized way while dealing with strings.

  Code:

  ```python
  from collections import deque
  s = 'python'
  d = deque(s)
  d.append('y')
  d.appendleft('h')
  print d
  d.pop()
  d.popleft()
  print list(reversed(d))
  ```

  Output:

  ```
  deque(['h', 'p', 'y', 't', 'h', 'o', 'n', 'y'])
  ['n', 'o', 'h', 't', 'y', 'p']
  ```

- **Sort using keys:** You can use the key parameter of built-in sorting, which is a faster way to sorting

Code:

```
list = [1, -3, 6, 11, 5]
list.sort()
print list

s = 'python'
s = sorted(s)
print s
```

Output:

```
[-3, 1, 5, 6, 11]
['h', 'n', 'o', 'p', 't', 'y']
```

- **Optimize loop:** You should write your code with timing parameters in your mind, particularly when dealing with loops. Because Python is designed to have only one way to do task.

Code:

```python
s = 'pythonprogram'
slist = ''
for i in s:
    slist = slist + i
print slist

# string concatenation
st = 'pythonprogram'
slist = ''.join([i for i in s])
print slist

# Better way to iterate a range
evens = [ i for i in xrange(10) if i%2 == 0]
print evens

# Less faster
i = 0
evens = []
while i < 10:
    if i %2 == 0:
        evens.append(i)
        i += 1
print evens

# slow
v = 'for'
s = 'python ' + v + ' python'
print s

# fast
s = 'python %s python' % v
print s
```

Output:

```
pythonprogram
pythonprogram
[0, 2, 4, 6, 8]
```

- **Try multiple methods in coding:** Always try multiple approaches while creating an application because one may give you better results than another. For the different inputs, it takes different times for execution. For some particular set of inputs, your chosen solution may be slow, you can decide as per your application need.

Code:

```python
my_dict = {'p':1,'r':1,'o':1,'g':1}
word = 'pythonprogram'
for w in word:
    if w not in my_dict:
        my_dict[w] = 0
    my_dict[w] += 1
print my_dict

# faster
my_dict = {'p':1,'r':1,'o':1,'g':1}
word = 'pythonprogram'
for w in word:
    try:
        my_dict[w] += 1
    except KeyError:
        my_dict[w] = 1
print my_dict
```

Output:

```
{'a': 1, 'g': 2, 'h': 1, 'm': 1, 'o': 3, 'n': 1, 'p': 3, 'r': 3, 't': 1, 'y': 1}
{'a': 1, 'g': 2, 'h': 1, 'm': 1, 'o': 3, 'n': 1, 'p': 3, 'r': 3, 't': 1, 'y': 1}
```

- **Use *xrange*:** This function is used to display a number by looping because it returns the generator object. This function is used to display only particular range on demand and hence it is known as "lazy evaluation". But it can save your system memory because it will yield only integer element at a time.

Code:

```
# slower
x = [i for i in range(0,10,2)]
print x

# faster
x = [i for i in xrange(0,10,2)]
print x
```

Output:

```
[0, 2, 4, 6, 8]
[0, 2, 4, 6, 8]
```

- **Use local variable:** Python retrieves local variable faster than retrieving global variable. Avoid global variable as much as you can. If you are accessing any statement often, which is inside a loop, then write it to a variable.

Code:

```
# run faster
class Test:
    def func(self,x):
        print x+x

Obj = Test()
my_test = Obj.func # Declaring local variable
n = 2
for i in range(n):
    my_test(i) # faster than Obj.func(i)
```

- **Lambda Function:** Lambda function is an anonymous function that can be used with *filter* (), *map* () and *reduce* () function.

Code:

```
>>> f =lambda x,y: x/y
>>> f(1,1)
1
>>>
```

Filter () –

Syntax:

> filter (function, list)

First parameter of "filter" is function and another is list.

Code:

```
>>> f =lambda x,y: x/y
>>> f(1,1)
1
>>> a = [1,2,3,4]
>>> p = map(lambda x:x*10, a)
>>> print p
[10, 20, 30, 40]
>>> a = [10,20,30,40,50,60]
>>> p = filter(lambda x: x % 2,a)
>>> print p
[]
>>> a = [1,2,3,4,5,6,7,8,9,10]
>>> p = filter(lambda x: x % 2,a)
>>> print p
[1, 3, 5, 7, 9]
>>>
```

Map () –

Syntax:

map (function, list)

First parameter of "map" is function and another is list.

Code:

```
>>> f =lambda x,y: x/y
>>> f(1,1)
1
>>> a = [1,2,3,4]
>>> p = map(lambda x:x*10, a)
>>> print p
[10, 20, 30, 40]
>>>
```

Reduce () –

Syntax:

reduce (function, list)

First parameter of "reduce" is function and another is list.

Code:

```
>>> a = range(2,6)
>>> p = reduce(lambda x,y:x+y, a)
>>> print p
14
>>>
```

- **List:** Use list instead of lengthy code. As it gives you the flexibility to eliminate a large number of lines from the program

Code:

```
>>>  q = [ ]
  File "<stdin>", line 1
    q = [ ]
    ^
IndentationError: unexpected indent
>>> q = [ ]
>>> for i in range(5,10):
...     for j in range(i*2,20):
...         q.append(j)
...
>>> print q
[10, 11, 12, 13, 14, 15, 16, 17, 18, 19, 12, 13, 14, 15, 16, 17, 18, 19, 14, 1
 16, 17, 18, 19, 16, 17, 18, 19, 18, 19]
>>>
```

Optimized way:

```
>>> a= [j for i in range(5,10) for j in range(i*2,100)]
```

- **Dictionary:** Use dictionary comprehension for optimization while creating a dictionary.

Code:

```
>>> d = {k: k*3 for k in range(1,5)}
>>> print d
{1: 3, 2: 6, 3: 9, 4: 12}
>>>
```

- **Use Import in proper manner:** Sometimes you need a particular package for a particular module so it is an optimized way if you specify particular package and module.

Code:

```
Normal way: from country import *
Correct way: from country.india import states
```

- **Lazy Generator:** If you are using range for finding some of 100 elements, then it will be waste of memory. You can use *xrange* for optimization, as it generates each number in which sum will consume to accumulate the sum.

Code:

```
>>> n=sum(range(100))
>>> print n
4950
>>> █
```

- **Peephole Technique:** It is a technique which is used to optimize small segments of instruction from a program. The segment is called as 'Peephole' or 'window'. It spots the instructions you can replace with minified program or instruction.

Code:

```
>>> ele = 'peephole'
>>> if ele in {'peephole', 'demo', 'optimization'} : print("TRUE")
...
TRUE
>>> █
```

In this example, we used the "in" operator to find particular elements from the collection. Here, Python detects that the collection will be used to verify the membership of the element. So it treats these instructions as a constant operation regardless of the size of the collection and it processes faster than tuples and lists. This method is also known as membership test in Python.

- **Use Advance profile with C Profile:** C profile is a part of packages in the Python programming. You can use C profile in many ways with your Python code. For example, you can wrap a function inside run method to measure performance of the program or run the script from command line with c profile as an argument.

Code:

```
>>> ele = 'peephole'
>>> if ele in {'peephole', 'demo', 'optimization'} : print("TRUE")
...
TRUE
>>> import cProfile
>>> cProfile.run('10*10')
         2 function calls in 0.000 seconds

   Ordered by: standard name

   ncalls  tottime  percall  cumtime  percall filename:lineno(function)
        1    0.000    0.000    0.000    0.000 <string>:1(<module>)
        1    0.000    0.000    0.000    0.000 {method 'disable' of '_lsprof.Prof
iler' objects}

>>>
```

You can look at a result and find out the area where you think you need to improve. You can attach C profile while running script too.

- **Interpret C Profile result:** It is even more important to find the culprit in analyzing the output. If you are able to find key element which constitute the CProfile report, then only you can make decision.

194

1. ncalls – Number of calls made.

2. tottime – time spent in given function.

3. percall – Represent quotient of "tottime" divided by "ncalls".

4. Cumtime – cumulative time in executing function.

5. filename_lineno (function) – Point of action in a program.

- **Optimization using IF statement:** Most of the programming languages allow for laziness – if evaluated, Python does, too. This means that if you add the "AND" condition, not all of the conditions will be tested when anyone is true unless it is an error.

  You can utilize this technique by normal adjustments of your current code. For example, if you are searching for a specific pattern in a program then you can reduce the scope with the use of "AND" condition.

Exercise

1. How does memory management works?

   Answer: Python memory is managed by Python's private heap space. All Python objects and data structures are in a private heap. Programmers do not have permission to access this private heap; the interpreter is responsible for handling this Python private heap.

   The Python heap space allocation for Python objects is done by the Python memory manager. The core API provides some tools for programmers to write code. Python also has a built-in garbage collector that reclaims all unused memory and frees memory and makes it available for heap space.

2. Why all memory is not de-allocated in Python?

Answer: Whenever Python exits, especially those Python modules that have circular references to other objects or objects referenced from the global namespace are not always de-allocated or freed. On exit, due to its own efficient cleanup mechanism, Python will try to release / destroy all other objects.

Chapter 15

Useful Python Libraries

Throughout this book, we have discussed various features of the Python language and its utilities, there are almost limitless uses of Python currently. Its uses in the various domains are due to its quick and easy programming approaches. Various libraries present until the date, enrich its usability. You could name any domain for programming and its libraries are available on the internet. It is just matter of importing those libraries in your code and using its modules for your program application.

We already discussed Python libraries related to mathematical and scientific application in "Mathematical Aspects". Let's see some more Python libraries and its applications a more in-depth. Meanwhile, you will get to know many ways to use it for your programming tasks. Let's get started!

Tkinter Library:

This library is built-in present with all the Python packages, so you don't need to install it separately on your system. As we have discussed in the chapter "_____". Tkinter's name is shorthand name for interface to Tk. This is one of the many GUI libraries for Python. To import this library into your program, you can use the following line:

$ import Tkinter

Or

$ from Tkinter import *

In case if you want to include only some module from it, you can use:

$ from Tkinter import moduleName

Where moduleName is any module name present in the Tkinter, the available modules are discussed in the further sections.

Uses:

You can use it to create your Graphical User Interfaces such as forms, button, checkboxes, and many other GUI features. Front-end designing is important aspects when creating any application. This library helps you in it.

Modules:

ScrolledText: to create a text widget having a scrollbar with it.

tkColorChooser: It allows the user to select a particular color.

tkCommonDialog: to create dialog box of different types.

tkFileDialog: To provide a dialog box to select or save the file by the user.

tkFont: To use the different font for GUI.

tkMessageBox: To create message boxes.

tkSimpleDialog: It provide primary dialog box functions.

PyQT Library:

PyQt is the most popular graphical user interface libraries, which is developed by Riverbank Computing Ltd. The library is used not only for computer applications, but also in embedded applications. There are many version of PyQT has been released.

To import this library in your code, you need to install PyQT using pip installer on your system.

Uses:

The uses of PyQT library are diverse. Some of the very complex applications (including Embedded Applications) using it for the development of their graphical user interface.

Modules:

There are hundreds of modules available from PyQT library; you just need to use particular modules as per your applications. You can go to the link for exploring its documentation:

http://pyqt.sourceforge.net/Docs/PyQt5/

Some of the general PyQt modules are as follows:

QtGui: It is used for system integration, handling GUI events, 2-dimensional graphics, basic images, text, and fonts.

QtWidgets: This module comprises of almost all classic user interface elements such as button, textbox, list wheel, etcetera.

QtFileDialog: This module contains all the classes and function related to selection and saving of files by the user.

Requests Library:

Requests is a very simple and quick HTTP library which was developed by Kenneth Reitz. It is the must known library for any Python programmer. Its beloved features attract every web Python developer.

To install it on your system and use it with your Python program, you need to setup it using pipenv.

Uses:

This library is useful for requesting URL in an automated way. There are various features available with it, such as network pooling, connecting to international domains and URLs, browser type SSL verification, and automatic decoding of content.

Modules:

Request: this method helps in sending a request to URL specified with it.

Head: this method is used to send the HEAD request.

Get: this method sends a GET Request.

Put: this method helps in sending PUT request.

Patch: this method is used to send PATCH request to URL.

Delete: this method is used to send DELETE request.

Exception:

There are many exceptions that occur while working with requests library. Let's understand these exceptions and there causes:

RequestException: Whenever there are ambiguous exceptions during the request.

ConnectionError: Whenever there is connection error occurs.

URLRequired: Whenever the correct URL is required for requesting.

ConnectionTimeout: Whenever a timeout occurs when connecting to a remote server.

HTTPError: Whenever HTTP error occurs.

SQLAlchemy Library:

It is one of the important Python database access libraries. It includes all the tools required for accessing SQL database and mapping to it. It provides flexibility and power to the developer for writing high-performance and efficient database program.

There are many advanced level database access functions available in this module. To install this library on your system, you need to take help from pip module.

Uses:

The fundamental utility of SQLAlchemy is to link your Python application to SQL database and access it using all the powers of SQL. The most popular feature of the SQLAlchemy library is ORM (Object-Relational Mapper). It is an optional component provided by this library which gives the data mapper pattern that allows your program to map to the database in multiple ways. If you want to explore more of its uses, you can visit http://www.sqlalchemy.org/

Modules:

SQLAlchemy has a rich set of modules in it, which gives your power to link and access SQL data in a flexible way. Some of its modules are as follows:

Query: Query is the basic source of all the SELECT statements in the SQL database. This method allows you to generate a query for the database.

Add_column: It helps in adding a column expression with the list of query results.

Add_Columns: It helps in adding multiple column expression with the list of query results.

Add_entity: It adds a mapped entry in the list of result.

All: it helps in returning results generated by the query.

As_scalar: It returns the whole SELECT expression given by the query.

Autoflush: It gives a query with particular set of "autoflush"

Column_description: it returns meta-data for the returned query column.

Count: It gives a count of rows from the returned query results.

Delete: it helps in deleting the bulk data from the query results.

RASPBERRY PI

Step-by-Step Guide To Mastering
Raspberry PI 3 Hardware and Software

Richard Ray

TABLE OF CONTENTS

Chapter 1

Introduction to Raspberry Pi

What you will learn in this chapter:

Raspberry Pi boards

Raspberry Pi hardware

What you will need for this chapter:

Raspberry Pi board

The Raspberry Pi was developed to encourage children who want to learn about computers and programming. The Raspberry Pi is one of the most popular devices in the system-on-a-chip (SoC) market, thanks to its rapid development and the low cost, which starts from just $5 for the Raspberry Pi Zero model. In 2015, more than five million

Raspberry Pi boards were sold. The Raspberry Pi boards are very complex, but the ability of the Raspberry Pi to run embedded Linux makes the device both powerful and accessible. Using Linux on embedded systems makes the development very easy, especially if we develop applications for smart things, the Internet of Things (IoT), robotics, smart cities, and cyber-physical systems. Thanks to the integration between Linux software and electronics, this board represents a paradigm shift in the development of embedded systems. You can use the Raspberry Pi not only in embedded systems development but also as a general purpose computer.

As we said before, the Raspberry PI can be used as a general purpose computing device. Because of that reason, it may be used to introduce computer programming to its users, but most of the developers use it as an embedded Linux platform.

Most of the Raspberry Pi models have the following features:

- Low cost, starting from $5 to $35

- Contains a powerful 1.2 GHz ARM Cortex – A53 processor which can process more than 700 million instructions per second

- Has many models that are suitable for different applications

- They save a lot of power since they run at 0.5W to 5.5W

- If you need support for any project, you can easily find a solution thanks to the huge community of innovators

- It can run a Linux operating system, so you can install open source libraries and many applications directly to it

It has Hardware Attached on Top (HATs)

This actually an impressive feature because you can extend the Raspberry Pi functionality using HAT that then connects to the GPIO

7

header, so you can design your own HATs and attach them to your Raspberry Pi header.

If you want to learn about electronics, programming, and the Linux operating system, you should use the Raspberry Pi platform especially for IoT applications and robotics.

The Raspberry PI is better than other embedded Linux devices and more traditional embedded systems, such as the Arduino, AVR, and PIC microcontrollers, is when you use Linux for your project. For example, if we develop a smart home system using the Raspberry Pi and you want to make information on the Internet, you can use and install the Nginx web server. After that, you can use a server-side language like PHP, Python, Perl, or any other programming language you may prefer. Also, you may want remote shell access, so you could install a Secure Shell without any effort by using the command: sudo apt install sshd. This will save you time.

On Linux operating systems you will find device driver support for many USB peripherals that makes the installation of any USB device so easy like camera, Wi-Fi adapters, and much more, instead of complex software drivers.

The Raspberry Pi can also play HD videos because it has a Broadcom BCM2835/6/7 processor used for multimedia applications, and it also a has a hardware implementation of H.264 MIPG-4 and MPG-2/VC-1 decoders and encoders.

If you are going to develop applications for a real time system then the Raspberry Pi will not be a good choice. For example, if you want to use a sensor to get some values every on millions of a second, it will be not easy to interrupt the system, but you can connect them with real-time micro-controllers through the buses like UART, 12C and Ethernet.

Raspberry Pi Hardware

The heart of every Raspberry Pi board is the Broadcom BCM2835, BCM2836, and BCM2837 system-on-a-chip (SoC). Raspberry Pi models are available for example (the Raspberry Pi A+, B+, 2, 3 and Zero), but I recommend purchasing the Raspberry Pi 3 because it has a multi-core processor.

Raspberry Pi Versions

● If you want to use the Raspberry Pi as a general purpose computer, you should consider the Raspberry Pi 3. The 1 GB of memory and 1.2 GHz processor provides the best performance compared to the other boards.

● For applications that interface electronics to the Internet on a network, use the Raspberry Pi 3 2 or Raspberry Pi B+.

● If you want a small board with wireless capability , the best choice would be the Raspberry Pi Zero

Model	RPi 3	RPi 2	RPi B+	RPi A+	RPi Zero	RPi B	Compute
Characteristics	performance/Wi-Fi Bluetooth/Ethernet	performance/Ethernet	Ethernet	price	price/size	original	integration/eMMC
Price	$35	$35	$25	$20	$5+	$25	$40 ($30 volume)
Processor*	BCM2837 quad core	BCM2836 quad core	BCM2835	BCM2835	BCM2835	BCM2835	BCM2835
	Linux ARMv7	Linux ARMv7	Linux ARMv6	Linux ARMv6	Linux ARMv6	Linux ARMv6	Linux ARMv6
Speed	1.2 GHz	900 MHz	700 MHz	700 MHz	1 GHz	700 MHz	700 MHz
Memory	1 GB	1 GB	512 MB	256 MB	512 MB	512 MB	512 MB
Typical power	2.5 W (up to 6.5 W)	2.5 W (up to 4.1 W)	1 W (up to 1.5 W)	1 W (up to 1.5 W)	1 W (up to 1.5 W)	1 W (up to 1.5 W)	1 W (up to 1.5 W)
USB Ports	4	4	4	1	1 OTG	2	via header
Ethernet	10/100 Mbps, Wi-Fi, and Bluetooth	10/100 Mbps	10/100 Mbps	none	none	10/100Mbps	none
Storage	micro-SD	micro-SD	micro-SD	micro-SD	micro-SD	SD	4 GB eMMC
Video	HDMI	HDMI	HDMI	HDMI	mini-HDMI	HDMI	HDMI via edge
	composite	composite	composite	composite	composite	RCA video	TV DAC via edge
Audio	HDMI digital audio and analog stereo via a 3.5 mm jack (where available)						via edge connector
GPU	Dual Core VideoCore IV Multimedia Co-Processor at 250 MHz (24 GFLOPS)						
Camera (CSI)	yes	yes	yes	yes	no	yes	CSI x 2 via edge
Display (DSI)	yes	yes	yes	yes	no	yes	DSI x 2 via edge
GPIO header	40 pins	40 pins	40 pins	40 pins	40 pins	26 pins	48 pins via edge
Usage	General-purpose computing and networking. High-performance interfacing. Video streaming	General-purpose computing. High-performance interfacing. Video streaming	General-purpose computing. Internet-connected host. Video streaming	Low-cost general-purpose computing. Standalone electronics interfacing applications	Low-cost small-profile standalone electronics interfacing projects	General-purpose legacy applications. Internet-connected host	Suitable for plugging into user-created PCBs using a DDR2 SODIMM connector. Open-source breakout board available

Details in this table were gleaned from articles and documents from the RPi Foundation website (www.raspberrypi.org)

* The BCM2835 is an ARM1176JZF-S (ARM11 processor architecture) that has full entitlement to an ARMv6 software architecture. The BCM2836 is a quad-core ARM Cortex-A7 processor that has a NEON Data Engine and full entitlement to an ARMv7 software architecture. The BCM2837 is a 64-bit ARMv8 quad-core ARM Cortex-A53 processor that has a NEON Data Engine and full entitlement to an ARMv7 software architecture.

Now let's take a closer look of the Raspberry hardware.

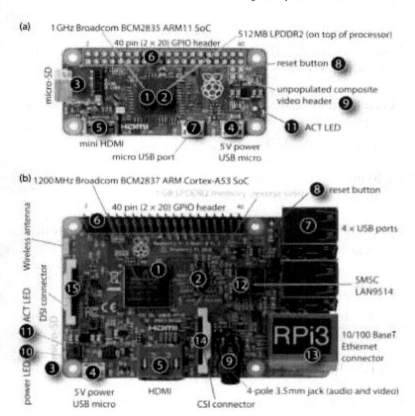

1. Processor: The Raspberry Pi uses the Broadcom BCM2835/BCM2836/BCM2837 processor.

2. Memory: The amount of system memory affects performance and the use of the Raspberry Pi as a general purpose computer. Memory is shared between the CPU and GPU (256 MB to 1GB DDR).

3. Storage: The Raspberry PI boards all boot from a micro SD or SD card, with the exception of the computer module. It has an on-board eMMC, which is effectively an SD card on a chip. The Raspberry PI 3 uses a friction-fit slot, rather than a click in/click out slot

4. Power: A 5v supply is required that can ideally deliver a current of at least 1.1A and 2.5A for the Raspberry Pi 3. Be careful not to continue the USB hub and USB power inputs on the Raspberry Pi Zero.

5. Video Out: Used to connect the Raspberry Pi boards to a monitor or television. The Raspberry Pi models support 14 output resolutions, including full-HD (1920 x 1080) and 1920 x 1200.

6. GPIOs: 40 pins that are multiplexed to provide access to the following features (2x I2C, SPI bus, UART, PWM, GPCLIK).

7. USB: There is an internal USB hub on Raspberry Pi models with varying numbers of inputs.

8. Reset: Can be used to reset the Raspberry Pi.

9. Audio and video: This provides composite video and stereo audio on the Raspberry PI.

10. Power LED: Indicates that the board is powered.

11. Activity LED: Indicates that there is activity on the board.

12. USB to Ethernet: This IC provides a USB 2.0 hub and a 10/100 Ethernet controller.

13. Network: 10/100 Mbps Ethernet via a RJ45 connector.

14. Camera: The Raspberry Pi has a mobile industry processor interface camera serial interface, a 15-pin connector that can be connected to a special purpose camera.

15. Display: The Display Serial Interface is an interface that is typically used by mobile phone vendors to interface with a screen display.

Questions for Chapter 1

1. What is the Raspberry Pi?

2. Describe the difference between the different Raspberry PI boards.

3. What are the HATs?

4. Describe the usage of the display on the Raspberry Pi.

5. Is the Raspberry Pi board good for real time system? Why or why not?

Chapter 2

Getting Started with the Raspberry Pi

What you will learn in this chapter:

📟 Understanding Linux

📟 Raspberry Pi software

What you will need for this chapter:

📟 Raspberry Pi board

USB cable

Micro-SD card

Serial cable or Wi-Fi adapter

Linux has many distributions (also known as versions) of its operating system. There are many different Linux versions such as Debian, Red Hat, or OpenSUSE that are mainly used on servers, but versions like Ubuntu, Fedora, or Linux Mint are used for desktop users. But you should keep in mind that they all have the same Linux kernel that was created by Linus Torvalds in 1991.

For an embedded system we will choose a distribution based on the following:

- The stability of the distribution

- The package manger

- The level of community support for the device used

- The device drivers support

Linux for the Raspberry Pi

As we said before that every Linux version has its own tools and configurations that result in a quite different user experience, the main open source Linux versions used on the Raspberry Pi board include Raspbian, Arch Linux, and Ubuntu.

Raspbian is a version of Debian; there are three versions of Raspbian on the Raspberry Pi website:

- **Raspbian Jessie:** An image based on Debian version 8.

- **Raspbian Jessie Lite:** A minimal image based on Debian Jessie, but with limited desktop support.

- **Raspbian Wheezy:** An older image based on Debian version 7.

- The Ubuntu distro (a distribution) is very close to Debian as described on the Ubuntu website "Debian is the rock upon which Ubuntu is built."

- Ubuntu is one of the most popular distributions because it has excellent desktop driver support, is easy to install, and is more accessible to new users.

- Arch Linux is a lightweight Linux version targeting competent Linux users. Prebuilt versions of the Arch Linux distribution are available for the Raspberry Pi, but it has less support for new Linux users that use the Raspberry Pi platform.

- The Raspberry Pi Foundation developed a Linux installer called NOOBS. It contains Raspbian but also provides the download and installation of other Linux distributions as well.

Let's create a Linux SD card image for the Raspberry PI

- If you want to set up an SD card to boot the Raspberry Pi, just download a Linux distribution image file from www.raspberrypi.org/downloads and write it to an SD card using any image writer.

Connect to a Network

There are two ways to connect the Raspberry Pi to a network using regular Ethernet or an Ethernet crossover cable.

Advantages	Disadvantages
You will have control over IP address settings	You will need administrative control
You can connect many boards	You will need a source power for the Raspberry Pi over Ethernet
The Raspberry Pi can connect to the Internet without a desktop computer	The setup is more complex for beginners

● The first thing you should do is find your Raspberry Pi on the network. By default, the Raspberry Pi request a Dynamic Host Configuration Protocol (DHCP) IP address. This service is provided by the DHCP server that runs on the integrated modem – router –LAN.

You can use any of the following methods to get the Raspberry Pi's dynamic IP address:

● Using a web browser: write 192.168.1.1, 192.168.0.1 or 10.0.0.1. Log in and look under the menu "Status" for the DHCP Table. You should see an entry with the details for the IP address, the MAC address, and the lease time remaining for a device with the hostname Raspberry Pi.

● Using a port scanning tool: Use a tool such as nmap under Linux or the Zenmap GUI version available for Windows. You will search for an entry has an open port 22 for SSH. It identifies the range of MAC addresses to the foundation. You can ping it to test the network connection.

Let's use the other type which is the Ethernet crossover cable

An Ethernet crossover cable is a cable that has been modified to enable similar devices to connect without using a switch.

Advantages	Disadvantages
In case you don't have access to the network , you can still connect the Raspberry Pi	When your desktop machine has only one network adapter, you will lose access to the Internet
Raspberry Pi can have Internet access if you have two network adapters and sharing is enabled	Raspberry Pi will need a source of power
You will have a stable network setup	You may need a specialized crossover cable

Here are the steps when you use the Windows operating system

1. Plug one end of the cable into the Raspberry Pi and the other end into the laptop socket.

2. Turn on the Raspberry Pi by attaching the micro-USB power supply.

3. Open up the Control Panel, choose Network Connections, then select two network adapters (wired and wireless). At the same time, right click and choose bridge connection.

4. Restart the Raspberry Pi. You can use a USB or TTL serial cable to do this, or use the reset button directly, then your Raspberry Pi will get an IP address from the DHCP server.

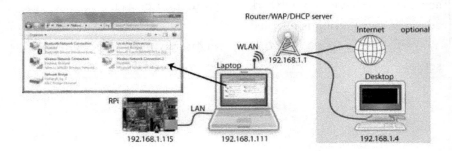

Communicating with Raspberry Pi

After you networked the Raspberry PI, the next thing that you will need to do is communicate with the Raspberry Pi. You can connect the Raspberry Pi using a serial connecting over USB to TTL or using a network connection as we did before. It is a fallback communication method for when something goes wrong with the software services on the Raspberry Pi board. You can also use it to configure wireless networking on the Raspberry Pi.

To connect the Raspberry pi through the serial connection, you will need terminal software; you can choose PuTTY or RealTeerm on Windows. If you are using a Linux OS, press Ctrl + Alt+T then type gnome-terminal under Debian.

To find the port number, open the Windows Device Manager, and find where the device is. It is listed as COMx.

Set up the connection speed; by default it will be 115,200 baud to connect the Raspberry Pi.

Then set the following values: bits = 8; Stop bits=1; Parity=none; and Flow control = XON/.XOFF.

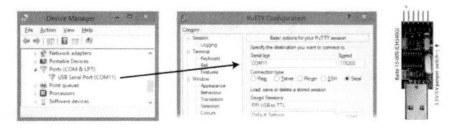

Connecting the Raspberry PI via SSH

Secure Shell (SSH) is a useful network protocol for secure encrypted communication between network devices. The SSH is running on port 22, and you can also use Putty to connect the Raspberry PI via SSH.

Basic Linux Commands

Command	Description
More/etc/issue	Returns the Linux Version
pp –p $$	Returns the shell you are suing (like bash)
whoami	Returns who you are logged in as
uptime	Returns how long the system has been running
top	Lists all of the processes and programs executing

File system Commands

Name	Command	Information	Example

List files	ls	Show all files	ls –alh
Current directory	pwd	Show the working directory	pwd -p
Change directory	cd	Change directory	cd /
Make a directory	mkdir	Create a directory	mkdir new
Delete directory	rm	Delete directory	rm new
Copy a directory	cp	Recursive copy	cp new new2
Create an empty file	touch	Create an empty file	touch f.txt
Get the calendar	cal	Display the calendar	cal 7 2017

Questions for Chapter 2

1. Describe some of Linux's features.

2. What is the SSH protocol?

3. List the advantages and disadvantages for the crossover Ethernet cable.

4. Which command you will use to show the current working directory?

Chapter 3

Introduction to Embedded Linux

What you will learn in this chapter:

Raspberry Pi boards

What you will need for this chapter:

Understanding Embedded Linux

More Linux commands

Intro to Git

First of all, the term embedded Linux is technically not one hundred percent correct because there is no special Linux kernel for embedded systems; it's the same Linux kernel for any device.

When we use the term embedded Linux, we mean that we use the Linux operating system on embedded systems, but embedded has different characteristics for the general purpose computing devices such as the following:

- Embedded systems have specific and dedicated applications

- Have limited memory, power, and storage capability

- They are almost always part of a larger system that may be linked to sensors or actuators

- They are embedded in automobiles, airplanes, and medical devices

- Works in real time (the outputs are directly related to its present inputs)

You can see embedded systems everywhere in everyday life. They can be found in vending machines, household appliances, smartphones, TVs, cars, parking systems, advanced driving assistance systems, and much more).

Advantages and disadvantages of Embedded Linux

- The Linux operating system is an efficient and scalable OS that can run on everything from low–cost devices to expensive large servers.

- Linux has a huge number of open source applications and tools.

- Open source = free.

- **Its only disadvantage** is that it cannot deal with real time applications due to the operating system overhead. So if you develop fast- response applications , like analog signal processing , embedded Linux will not be the best choice , but in special cases it can handle the real time systems using embedded Linux.

Booting the Raspberry Pi

If you boot your desktop computer, you will see the Unified Extensible Firmware Interface (UEFI), which provides legacy support for BIOS (Basic Input/Output System) services. The Boot menu displays the system information and you can change the setting by pressing any key. UEFI tests the hardware of your computers like the memory, the hard disk, and then loads the operating system from the solid state drive (SSD). When a desktop computer is powered on , the UEFI/BIOS performs these steps:

1. Takes control of the processor of your computer

2. Tests the hardware components

3. Loads the operating system from your hard drive

Raspberry Pi Bootloaders

Like any embedded Linux device, the Raspberry PI does not have a BIOS by default. Indeed, it uses a combination of Bootloaders. Bootloaders are programs used to link your hardware to your operating system.

- Check the controllers such as the memory, I/O

- Prepare the memory for the operating system

- Load the operating system passing the control to it

In the following illustration you can find the sequence of the booting process on the Raspberry Pi.

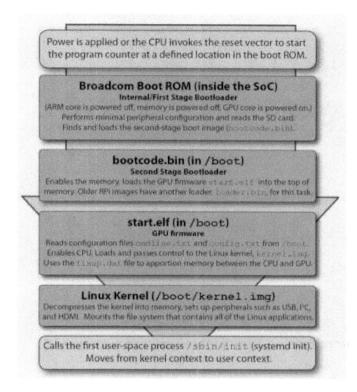

Power is applied or the CPU invokes the reset vector to start the program counter at a defined location in the boot ROM.

Broadcom Boot ROM (inside the SoC)
Internal/First Stage Bootloader
(ARM core is powered off, memory is powered off, GPU core is powered on.)
Performs minimal peripheral configuration and reads the SD card.
Finds and loads the second-stage boot image (bootcode.bin).

bootcode.bin (in /boot)
Second Stage Bootloader
Enables the memory, loads the GPU firmware start.elf into the top of memory. Older RPi images have another loader, loader.bin, for this task.

start.elf (in /boot)
GPU firmware
Reads configuration files cmdline.txt and config.txt from /boot.
Enables CPU. Loads and passes control to the Linux kernel, kernel.img.
Uses the fixup.dat file to apportion memory between the CPU and GPU.

Linux Kernel (/boot/kernel.img)
Decompresses the kernel into memory, sets up peripherals such as USB, I²C, and HDMI. Mounts the file system that contains all of the Linux applications.

Calls the first user-space process /sbin/init (systemd init).
Moves from kernel context to user context.

● Also, you can find the same information using the command dmesg | more in the terminal.

Kernel and User Space

● The kernel space is the area that the Linux kernel runs in. It's an area of the system memory, but the area that regular applications run in is called user space, and there is a hard boundary between the kernel and the user space; this is to prevent the kernel from crashing, in case the user wrote bad code.

● The Linux kernel has the full access of the physical recourse, including memory on the Raspberry PI board.

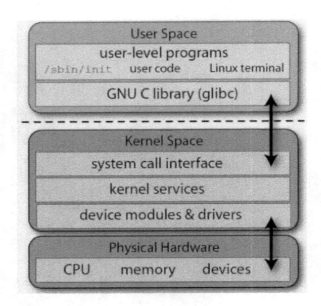

More commands on Linux (some system commands)

systemct1 : Lists all running services.

systemect1 start ntp: Starts a service. Does not persist after reboot.

systemct1 stop ntp: Stops a service. Does not persist after reboot.

systemct1 enable ntp: Enables a service to start on boot.

systemct1 disable ntp: Disables a service from starting on boot.

systemct1 reload ntp: Reloads configuration files for a service starting on boot.

• **The Super User** on Linux = the system administrator who has the highest level of security access to all commands. You can use the terminal as a super user by typing the **sudo passwd root** command.

29

Let's create a new user on the Raspberry Pi

Called USER

Open the terminal window and write the following commands:

pi@erpi- $ sudo adduser USER

Adding the user 'USER' . . .

Adding new group 'USER' (1002) . . .

 Adding new user 'USER' (1001) with group 'USER' . . .

Creating home directory '/home/USER' . . .

Copying files from 'etc/skel' . . .

Enter new UNIX password: enter your password

Retype new UNIX password: enter your password

Passwd: password updated successfully

Git version control

Git is a system that allows you to track your changes of the software you are developing.

There are two types of version control systems:

• Distributed: Like Git. Using such systems, you cannot pull down changes but you can clone the entire repository. "Clone" means copy, and it can become the master copy if required.

• Centralized: Like Apache (SVN), works on systems like that where you will find a master copy of your project, and then you can pull down changes.

For more details you can check out git.kernel.org

Questions for Chapter 3

1. What is embedded Linux?

2. Create a user called "your name" on the Raspberry Pi.

3. Describe the concept of version controls and its types.

4. List the sequence of the booting process on the Raspberry Pi.

Chapter 4

Working with Electronics

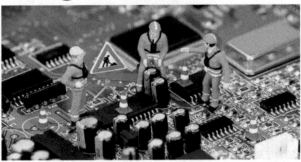

What you will learn in this chapter:

🏭Raspberry Pi boards

What you will need for this chapter:

🏭Understanding the basics of electronics components

🏭Interfacing electronics with the Raspberry Pi

Electronics components

Digital Multimeter

DMM is an electrical device used to measure the voltage, current, and resistance of a circuit.

If you don't have one, buy one that has the following features:

- **Auto range:** To automatically detect the range of the measurements.

- **Auto power off:** To save power and not waste your battery.

- **True RMS:** A multimeter with this feature uses real calculations to analyze phase-controlled devices like solid state drives.

Introduction to electric circuits

- **Ohm's Law→ V = I X R**

This is the most important equation you will need.

- **V** for **Voltage**. Voltage is the potential difference between two points on a circuit. For example, if you have a buffer tank of water which is connected to the tap, water will flow if you turn on the tap because the height of the tank and the gravity, but if the tap was at the same height as the top of the water tank, water wouldn't flow because in this case there is no potential energy. Voltage also exhibits the same behavior; if the one side has a higher voltage than the other side , the current will flow across the component.

- **I for Current.** Measured in amperes (A), current is the flow of the electrical charge. Like in the water tank example, the current will be the flow of the water from the tank to the tap.

- **R for Resistance** (R). Resistance is measured in ohms (Ω), and is something that reduces the flow of current through the dissipation of the power; power(P) in watts(W), P = V X I.

For example if you want to buy a resistor that limits the current to 100mA using a 5v supply, you can calculate it as the following $R = V$ $R/(IR = 5\ V)/(100\ mA) = \mathbf{50\ \Omega,}$ and the power will be $P = VI = 0.5W.$

- *The total resistance of the series resistors = R1 + R2 + ... + Rn*

- *The voltage across the same resistor V supply= Vr1 + Vr2 + ... + Vr3*

Let's implement Raspberry Pi circuits on a breadboard.

We will use a breadboard for prototyping circuits, and in the next circuit we will use two horizontal power rails for 3.3V and 5V power. The Raspberry Pi GPIO headers consist of male pins, so you will need to use female jumper connectors for wiring the circuit.

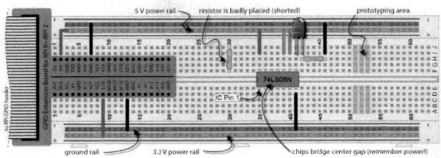

- Connect the circuit as shown in the above figure.

Digital multimeters and the breadboard

- We can measure the voltage on the circuit by connecting the multimeter in parallel (black probe in the COM).

- If you want to measure the current on the circuit you should insert the multi-meter between the components

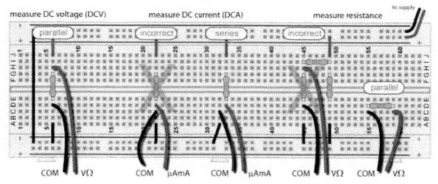

- A voltage regulator is a device that takes the varying input voltage and outputs a constant voltage, the Raspberry Pi B+ and Raspberry Pi 2/3 models have a dual efficiency PWM DC TO DC converter that can apply different fixed voltage levels on-board if there is a 5v, 3.3v and a 1.8v output. You can use the 5v and 3.3v on the Raspberry Pi GPIO headers, and the board can support up to 300mA on the 5v (pins 2 and 4).

And 50mA on the 3.3v pins (pins 1 and 17).

- If you want a larger current, you can use an external regulator which is used for components like motors.

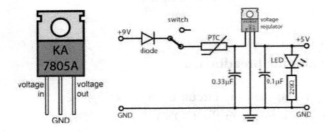

A diode is a semiconductor that allows the current to pass in one direction.

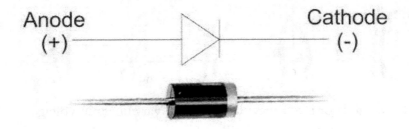

Light Emitting Diode (LED)

A light emitting diode is a semiconductor-based light source used mainly for debugging purposes.

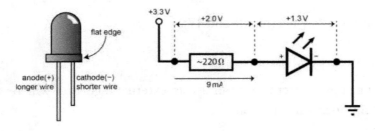

Capacitor

A capacitor is an electrical component used to store electrical energy.

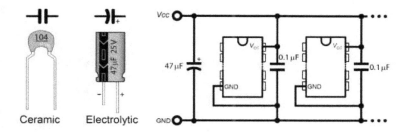

Ceramic   Electrolytic

- The first number is the first digit for the value.

- The second number is the second digit for the value.

- The third number is the number of zeros.

For example:

$104 = 100000\text{pF} = 100\text{nF} = 0.1\mu\text{F}$

Transistors

Transistors are one of the core components of any microprocessor or any electronic system. We use transistors to amplify a signal on or off. You can also use it as a switch.

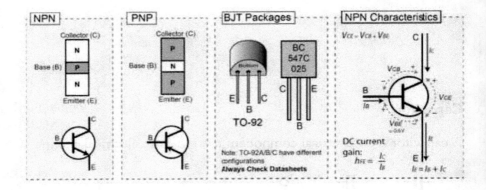

NPN

Collector (C)

N
Base (B)	P
N

Emitter (E)

PNP

Collector (C)

P
Base (B)	N
P

Emitter (E)

BJT Packages

BC
547C
025

C   E

E   C
B

TO-92

B

Note: TO-92A/B/C have different configurations
Always Check Datasheets

NPN Characteristics

$V_{CE} = V_{CB} + V_{BE}$

C
I_C

V_{CB}

B
I_B

V_{CE}

V_{BE}
$\approx 0.6V$

E
$I_E = I_B + I_C$

DC current gain:
$h_{FE} = \dfrac{I_C}{I_B}$

39

Questions for Chapter 4

1. Explain Ohm's Law.

2. What is resistance?

3. What are the benefits of using regulators?

4. Describe how a diode works.

Chapter 5

Programming a Raspberry Pi

What you will learn in this chapter:

📖Programming the Raspberry Pi using different languages

📖The difference between the compiler and interpreter

📖An intro to Python programming

What you will need for this chapter:

📖Raspberry Pi board

📖Resistors, a breadboard, LEDs, transistors

Introduction

In this chapter we will use many programming languages for the Raspberry Pi, including scripting and compiling languages. Take a look at the structure and syntax of each language and the advantages and disadvantages of each language (with examples), but we will mainly focus on the Python programming language.

Any programming language available on Linux will be also available on the Raspberry Pi , then you can choose the suitable language depending on the kind of application you are developing.

If you would like to do any of the following:

• Write device drivers for Linux

• Develop graphical user interfaces

• Design web applications

• Design a mobile application

Each choice will impact the option of the suitable language needed for that particular task, but there is a difference between the development for embedded systems and the development for other platforms like desktop, web, or mobile applications when you are developing for the embedded system. You should keep the following in mind:

● You should write clean code.

● You should optimize the code only if you complete it.

● You should have a good understanding of the hardware you are developing on.

Languages on the Raspberry Pi

By now you must be thinking, "What programming language should I use on the Raspberry Pi to guarantee the best performance?" Actually, this is a fairly difficult question to answer because, as we said before, it depends on what type of the application you are developing.

● Interpreted: The source code won't be translated directly to machine code, but the interpreter will read your code and then execute it line by line.

● Compiled: The compiler will translate the language directly to the machine code (0s and 1s).

● JIT: Just in time compiled means it has the feature of the compiled language, which is translating the source code directly into machine code. It also has the interpreter language, which is translated into the code line by line.

 Also you may use Cython, this allow you to generate C code from your Python code. We will show some examples using Cython and the extended version of Python.

Write the following commands on the terminal if you want to set the CPU frequency.

$sudo apt install cpufrequtils

$cpufreq-info

Set clock freq write the following commands.

$sudo cpufreq-set -g performance

$cpufreq-info

$sudo cpufreq-set –f 700MHz

$cpufreq-info

Example: Driving an LED with Raspberry Pi pins using transistors (wiring).

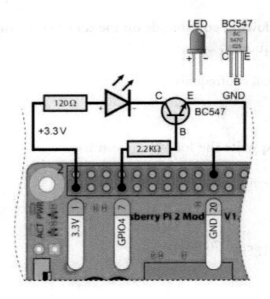

Example: Driving an LED with Raspberry Pi pins using transistors.

After wiring the circuit as shown, you can use Linux to control the Raspberry Pi pins with the following code:

```
$ cd /system/class/gpio

/system/class/gpio $ ls

/system/class/gpio $ echo 4 > export

/system/class/gpio $ ls

/system/class/gpio $ cd gpio4

/system/class/gpio/gpio4 $ ls
```

Now it's time to control GPIO4:

/system/class/gpio/gpio4 $ echo out > direction

/system/class/gpio/gpio4 $ echo 1 > value

/system/class/gpio/gpio4 $ echo 0 > value

A scripting language is a type of computer programming that is used to write scripts that are interpreted directly with no compiler.

There are many types like:

• **Python**: It's a great and very easy language to learn and use for scripting and object-oriented support features.

• **Bash**: A good choice for short tasks and you don't need advanced programming structures.

• **Perl**: You can use this language for text or process data. It allows you to write code in object-oriented paradigms.

• **Lua**: This scripting language is used a lot with embedded applications. It is a lightweight language and supports object-oriented programming styles.

Example: Drive the LED using Bash.

LED-IO = 5 # use a variable called LED with value 5

Function blinkLED

{

  Echo $1 >> "/sys/class/gpio/gpio$LED_IO/value"

}

If [$# -ne 1]; then

echo "No command has been entered".

echo " on or off "

echo –e " setup the LED "

exit 2

if

echo"The command has been entered is $1"

```
if ["$1" == "setup"]; then

echo "IO $1"

echo "the LED is on"

echo $LED_IO >> "sys/class/IO/export"

sleep 1

echo "away" >> "sys/class/IO$LED_IO/direction"

elif ["$1" == "on"]; then

echo "LED is on"

blinkLED 1

elif ["$1" == "off"]; then

echo "LED is off"

blinkLED 0

elif [$1 == "status"]; then

state=$(cat "/sys/class/IO/IO$LED/value")

echo "LED State is: $state"

elif ["$1" == "end"]; then

echo"Io num $LED_IO"

echo $LED_IO >> "/sys/class/IO/unexport"

fi
```

Example: Drive the LED using Lua.

```
local LED4_PIN = "sys/class/IO/IO4"

local SYSFS_DIR = "sys/class/IO/"

local LED_Num = "4"

function writeIO(dir, filen, val)

file = IO.open(dir..filen,"w")

file:write(val)

file:close()

end

print("Driving the LED")

ifarg[1] == nil then

print("you should enter a command")

print(" usage is: command")

print("1 -> on or 0-> off")

do return en

end

if arg[1] == "off" then

print("The LED is on")
```

```
wirteIO("LED4_PIN", "val", "1")

elseif arg[1] == "configure "then

print("the LED is off")

WirteIO(LED4_PIN, "val", "0")

Elesif arg[1] == "configure"

Print("configure the IO")

WriteIO(SYSFS_DIR, "xport", LED_NUM)

Os.execute()

WriteIO(LED4_PIN,"DIR","out")

Elseif arg[1]=="sta"then

Print("turn IO off"

Print("find the LED sta")

File=io.open(LED4_PIN.."val","r")

File:close()

Else

Print("please insert a valid command")

End

Print("the end")
```

Example: Drive the LED using Python.

```python
Import sys

From time import sleep

LED4_PIN = "/sys/class/IO/IO4"

SYS_DIR = "/sys/class/IO"

LED_NUM = "4"


def wLED(fname, val, PIN = LED4_PIN)

"This function to set the value on the file"

Fileo = open(PIN + fname,"w")

Fileo.write(val)

Fileo.close()

Return


Print("start the script")

If len(sys.argv) !=4

Print("incorrect argument")

Sys.exit(4)

If.argv[1]=="on"
```

```python
Print("the LED is on")

wLED(fname="val", val="1")

elif sys.argv[1] =="turn off"

 print("The LED is off")

wLED(fname="val", val="0")

elif sys.argv[1]=="configure":

print("configure the IO")

wLED(fname="xport", val="LED_NUM", PIN=SYS_DIR)

sleep(0.1)

wLED(fname="DIR", val="out")

eleif sys.argv[1] == "close"

print("The IO I off")

wLED(fname="unexport", val=LED_NUM, PIN=SYS_DIR)

eleif sys.argv[1]=="state"

print("the LED state")

fileo = open(LED4_PIN + "val", "r")

print(fileo.read())

fileo.close()

else

print("please enter a valid command")
```

```python
print("end of the script")
```

Questions of Chapter 5

1. What is the object-oriented paradigm?

2. Define the difference between compiled and interpreted languages.

3. Write python code to turn on an LED on GPIO 4 60 times in one minute.

Chapter 6

Input and output on a Raspberry pi

What you will learn in this chapter:

📖Interfacing on a Raspberry Pi

📖PWM concepts

📖The importance of pull up and pull down resistors

What you will need for this chapter:

📖Raspberry Pi board

📖Buttons, transistors

📖LEDs

Introduction

In this chapter you will use what you have learned in the five previous chapters about Linux, programming, and electronics basics, so you will start working with the general purpose inputs/outputs on the Raspberry Pi, as well as work with Pulse Width Modulation (PWM). At the end, you will work with the Wiring Pi Library, so let's get started...

After showing you how to administrate Linux and practice different commands on the command line, building electronic circuits, and programming using different languages it's now time to integrate all of these things to control the Raspberry Pi in different ways like:

● Using the buses, for example SPI and I2C.

● Using UART on the GPIO.

● Communicating through Wi-Fi or Bluetooth with electronic components.

● Connecting your USB devices like keyboards, Wi-Fi modules, etc.

Now we will use the GPIO header to connect the Raspberry Pi to circuits. The next example will provide you a view of the functions of the GPIO header, you will find that many of the pins are multiplexed, which means that the same pin can do more than one.

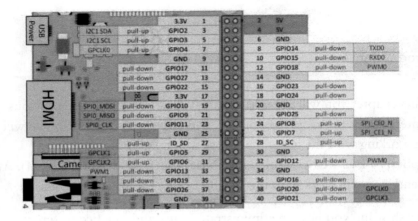

General Purpose Inputs/ Outputs

You can use them for the following purpose:

● **Digital input:** In this case, you can read a digital output from an electronic device/circuit.

● **Analog output:** You can use Pulse width modulation to output a signal that can be used as a voltage level to control devices like servo motors.

● **Digital output:** You can use a GPIO to turn the circuit on or to turn it off, for example when you use an LED or a relay (switch) to turn on/off high voltage devices.

● **Analog input:** You cannot use this feature (ADC) directly on the Raspberry Pi, but you can add it using bus devices.

General purpose input/output digital output

In this example we used a GPIO to connect a FET to the switch circuit.

57

When the voltage is applied to the gate, it will close the switch to enable the current to flow from 5 volts using the 220 ohm resistor. This is applied on the right-hand side picture, and you can use this circuit for many on/off output and input applications because the BS270FET can drive a constant current up to 400mA.

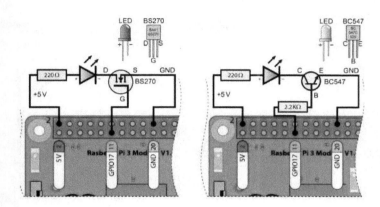

Now let's test the performance of this circuit using a short bash shell script to control the LED.

Write the following:

echo 17 > /sys/class/gpio/export

sleep 0.7

echo "" > /sys/class/gpio/gpio7/direction

count = 0

while [$count –lt 100000]; do

echo 1 > /sys/class/gpio/gpio17/val

let count = count +1

echo 0 > /sys/class/gpio/gpio17/value

done

echo 17 > /sys/class/gpio/unexport

This is the reading of output signal on an oscilloscope:

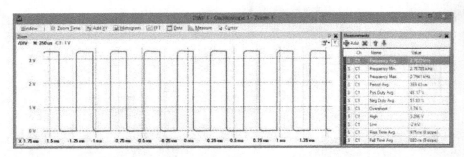

General purpose input/output digital input

In this example we will apply the concept of GPIO digital input.

The GPIO digital input will allow us to read the state of a pushbutton or any on/off input (0 or 1) we will use both the Linux terminal and C++ to perform this task. The circuit in the following figures use normal pushbuttons (SPST) that are connected to the Raspberry Pi pin 13/GPIO27. You will not need pull-up or pull-down resistors on pushbutton switches because pin 13 on the GPIO header is directly consented to ground using an internal resistor (pull down resistor).

Open the Linux terminal and write the following:

/sys/class/gpio/$ echo 27 >export

/sys/class/gpio/$ c gpio twenty seven

/sys/class/gpio/gpiotwentyseven $ ls

/sys/class/gpio/gpiotwentyseven $echo in > direction

/sys/class/gpio/gpiotwentyseven $ cat direction in

/sys/class/gpio/gpiotwentyseven $ cat value 0

/sys/class/gpio/gpiotwentyseven $ cat value 1

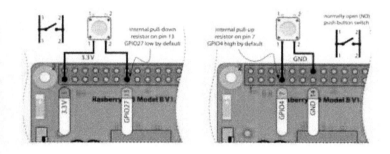

The pull down and pull up resistors

● **Pull up resistor**: From its name, it pulls the voltage of the wire that connected to its source when the other components on the line are inactive, and they are disconnected.

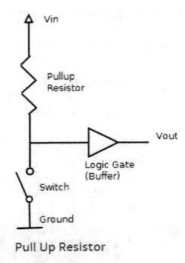

Vin

Pullup
Resistor

Vout

Logic Gate
(Buffer)

Switch

Ground

Pull Up Resistor

- **Pull down resistor:** It works like the pull up resistor, but it's connected to the ground and holds the signal when the other devices are disconnected.

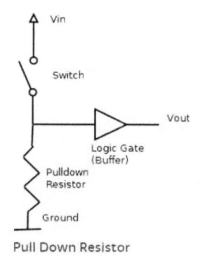

Pull Down Resistor

Control the GPIOs using C++

There is a C++ class with the sysfs GPIO functions on the Raspberry Pi to make it much easier to use. You transfer it to any embedded Linux device. There is another approach called memory-mapped that you will see at the end of the chapter, but keep in mind that all of these approaches are specific to the Raspberry Pi board.

#define GPIO_Address "/sys/class/gpio"

Namespace Raspberry {

enum GPIO_DIR {IN, OUT};

enum GPIO_VAL {low=0, HIGH=1};

enum GPIO_EDGE {none, rise, fall, both}

```
};


Class GPIO {

private:

int number, debounceTime;

string name, address;

public:

GPIO(int number);

Virtual int getNumber(){return number;}


// input and output configurations

Virtual int setDir(GPIO_DIR);

Virtual GPIO_DIR getDIR();

Virtual int setVal(GPIO_VAL);

Virtual int toggleOut();

Virtual GPIO_VAL getVal ();

Virtual int setActivelow(bool is low=true);

Virtual int setAciveHigh();

Virtual void setDebounceTime(int time)

{this-> debounceTime = time;
```

63

```cpp
}
};
// Advanced, faster by open the stream
Virtual int streamopen();

Virtual int streamWrite(GPIO_VAL);

Virtual int streamClose();

Virtual int toggleOut(int time);

Virtual int toggleOut(int numOfTime, int time);

Virtual void changeToggTime(int time)


{
  This->threadRunning =false;

}
// input
Virtual int setEdgeType(IO_EDGE);

Virtual IO_EDGE getEdge();

Virtual int waitEdge();

Virtual int waitEdge(callbackType callback);

Virtual void waitEdgeClose() {this->threadRunning = false;}

Virtual ~IO(); // destructor
```

```
Private:

Int write(string address, string fname, string val);

Int write (string address, string fname, int val);

string read(string address, string fname);

int exportIO();

int unexportIO();

of stream;

thr_t thread;

callbackType callbackfunc;

bool thrRunning;

int togglePer;

int toggleNum;

friend void* thrpoll(void *val);

};


Void* thrpoll(void *val);

Void* thrtogg(void *val);

}/* namespace Raspberry*/


File c++control.cpp
```

```cpp
#include<iostream>

#include<unistd.h> //for usleep function

#include"GPIO.h"

Using namespce Raspberry

Using namespace std;

Int main()

{

GPIO outIO(17);

outIO.setDIR(OUT);


for(int I =0; I <10; i++)

{

  outIO.setVal(HIGH);

usleep(400000);

outIO.setVal(LOW);

usleep(400000);

}

inIO.setDIR(INPUT);

cout << "input state is"<<inIO.getVal() <<endl;

outIOlstreamOpen()
```

```
for(int i =0; I < 100000000; i++)

{

  outIO.streamWrite(HIGH);

outIO.streamWrite(LOW);

}

outIO.close();

return 0;
```

In the following figure you will see the performance of the code when the write() method is used; it is flashing at 129 kHz.

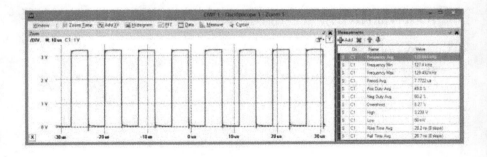

POSIX

Ptherads is a set of functions written in the C language to allow you to implement threads with C/C++ programs. You will need threads when you want to run some parts of your code at the same time.

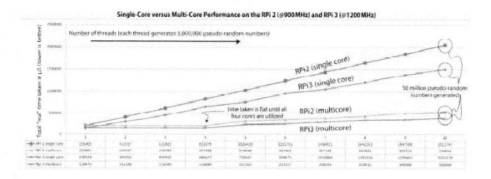

Pulse Width Modulation - LED Fading

The Raspberry Pi has the capability (PWM) to provide analog to digital conversion (DAC), which is usually used for motor devices.

All Raspberry Pi boards have Pulse Width Modulation pins.

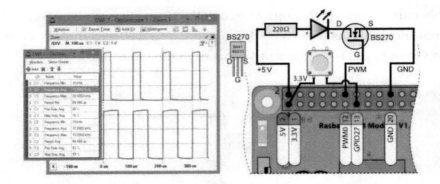

We will use the PWM feature to fade an LED by changing the duty cycle value.

Create file call LEDFading.cpp.

Then write the following code:

```cpp
#include <iostream>

#include <wiringPi.h>

#include <unistd.h>

Using namespace std;

#define LED_PIN 18

#define Button_PIN 27

Bool run  = true;

Void buttPress(void)
```

```
{
  Cout<< "you pressed the Button";

Run = false

}

Int main ()

{
  wiringPiSetupIO();

pinMode(LED_PIN, OUTPUT);

pinMode(Button_PIN, INPUT);

wirinPisr(Button_PIN, INT_EDGE_Rise, &buttPress);

cout << "LED fading until the button is pressed";

while(run)

{
  For (int I =1; I <=1023; i++)

{
  pmWrite(LED_PIN, i);

usleep(1000);

}
  for(int i=1022; i>=0; i--)

{
```

```
    pmWrite(LED_PIN, i);

usleep(1000);      //delay

}

}

return 0;

}


}
```

Questions for Chapter 6

1. Describe the difference between pull-up and pull-down resistors.

2. What is Pulse Width Modulation? How many pins are on the Raspberry Pi?

3. List the purposes of using the general input output pin on the Raspberry Pi.

4. Using C++, write a program to control servo motors using the PWM pin on the Raspberry Pi.

5. What is the benefit of using POSIX?

Chapter 7

Introduction to Communication Protocols

What you will learn in this chapter:

📖Understand bus communication

📖More code with C/C++

What you will need for this chapter:

📖Raspberry Pi board

📖Seven segment display

📖Shift register

Introduction

In this chapter you will work with the following communication protocols:

- SPI: serial peripheral interface

- I2C: inter integrated circuit

- UART: Universal Asynchronous Receiver/Transmitter

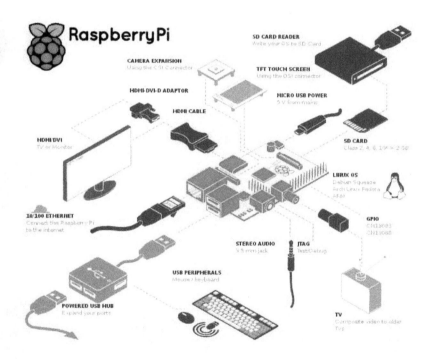

I2C

The I2C protocol or IIC is a protocol with two wires that were invented by the Philips company. The benefit of this protocol is to connect microcontrollers with other peripheral devices. You can use it with the Raspberry Pi for the following reasons::

• The Raspberry Pi will act as the master device.

• The other devices will connect to the Raspberry Pi and will act as slaves on the same wire.

The Advantages of using I2C

• You can implement the I2C using just two signal lines for communication, which is the serial data and the serial clock.

- **Serial data:** to transfer the data

- **Serial clock:** to synchronize the data transfer

• Any device on the bus can be a master or a slave.

- Master device: the device that can initiate communication

- Slave device: the device that can respond

• There is a built-in chip for noise filtering.

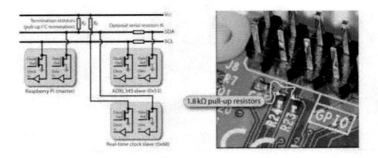

●On the Raspberry Pi, the IIC was implemented using the Broadcom controller, which supports up to 400,000 Hz. NXP has a new one which supports up to 1,000,000 Hz.

● You can see the pull up resistors on the serial data and the serial clock. They are used as termination resistors; they enable the master device to take control of the bus with the slaves.

To configure the I2C on the Raspberry Pi, open the terminal and write the following:

Config.txt | grep i2c_arm

Then save and restart; let's make it available.

After the restart, open the terminal and write the following:

Sudo modprobe i2c-bcm2708

Sudo modprobe i2c-dev

Lsmod | grep i2c

On the Raspberry Pi you will find the following I2C buses:

I2C1: Serial data on PIN3, Serial clock on PIN5, not enabled by default.

I2C0: Serial data on PIN27, Serial clock on PIN28, this is used for HAT management.

To change the baud rate, open the terminal and then write the following:

Sudo cat /sys/module/i2c_bcm2708/parameter/baudrate

Reboot and then write the following

Sudo cat /sys/module/i2c_bcm2708/parameter/baudrate 4000

I2C in C programming

This program can be run on any i2c device.

```
#include<stdio.h>

#include<fcnt1.h>

#include<sys/ioct1.h>

#include<Linux/i2c.h>

#include<Linux/i2c-dev.h>

#define size 19

Int bTOD (char b)

{

return (b/16)*10 + (b%16);

}
```

```c
Int main()

{

    Int file;

    Printf("test is starting \n");

    If(file=open("/dev/i2c-1", o_RDWR < 0)

    {

        perror(" cannot open your bus\n ");

        return 1;

    }

    If(ioctl(file, I2C_SLAVE, 0x68) < 0)

    {

    Perror ("cannot connect the sensor");

    Return 1;

    }

    Char writeBuff[1] = {0x00};

    If (write(file, writeBuff, 1)!=1

    {

    Perror("Failed to set your entered address\n");

    Return 1;

    }
```

```
Char buff(Size);

If(read(file, buff, Size)!=Size)

{

  Perror("Failed to your data in the buffer\n");

}

Printf("Time is %02d:%02d:%02d\n", bTOD(buff[0]));

Float temp = buff[0x11] + ((buff [0x12] >>6)*0.25);

Printf("the temp : %f\n", temp);

Close(file);

Return 1;

}
```

SPI BUS

SPI stands for Serial Peripheral Interface. It's a fast, full duplex serial data link that allows devices like the Raspberry Pi to communicate with other devices, but in short distances, so such as I2C the SPI Protocol is also synchronous. But I2c is not a full duplex bus unlike the SPI, so if you use SPI you can send and receive the data at the same time. We will use the SPI bus to drive a seven segment LED Display using an 8-bit shift register.

Now let's take a look at the differences between IIC and SPI.

IIC: Two wires, 128 devices can be attached. **SPI**: Four wires, and also needs to connect it with logic if you want to attach more than one slave device.

IIC: It uses half duplex with 400000Hz. **SPI**: It uses full duplex with 32MHz.

IIC: You will need to connect pull-up resistors. **SPI**: There is no need for pull-up resistors.

IIC: The most important feature is that you can have multiple masters. **SPI**: Very simple but no more than one master device.

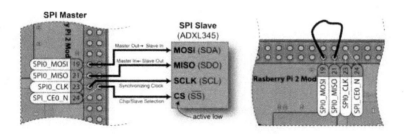

SPI bus works using one of the four modes that are chosen based on the specification defined in the data sheet of the SPI device. The data can be synchronized by the clock signal and any of the communication modes. The polarity can be defined if the clock is low or high.

SPI Modes

Mode: 0, **polarity**: 0 (low), **clock Phase**: 0

Mode: 1, **polarity**: 0 (low), **clock Phase**: 1

Mode: 2, **polarity**: 1 (high), **clock Phase**: 0

Mode: 3, **polarity**: 1 (high), **clock Phase**: 1

● There is no defined maximum data rate with the SPI protocol, also no flow control, and no communication acknowledgement.

Raspberry Pi and SPI Protocol

The GPIO header on the Raspberry Pi that has the SPI bus is disabled by default, but you can enable the bus by the following steps:

● Add an entry to the file /boot/config.txt/etc/modules

Cat config.txt | grep spi

Cat modules | grep spi

Sudo reboot

Ls spi*

SPI application (seven segment display)

The seven segment display consists of eight LEDs that can be used to display decimal or hexadecimal numbers. There are many types with different colors and sizes.

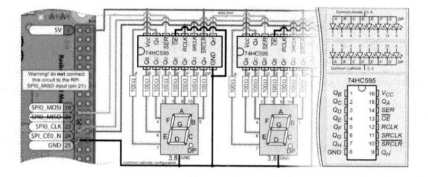

The 74HC595 can be connected to the Raspberry Pi board using three of the four SPI lines.

● Connect the SPI0_CLK to the Serial clock input (pin 11) of the 74HC595.

● The benefit of SPI0_MOSI is to transfer the data from the Raspberry Pi to the 74HC595 Serial input (pin 14). You can send 8 bits at a time.

● SPI_CE0_N is connected to the Register Clock input to latch the 74HC595 to the output pins to light the LEDs.

The SPI Communication in C programming

#include <stdio.h>

#include<cnt1.h>

#include<unistd.h>

#include<stdint.h>

```c
#include<linuxspi/spidev.h>

#define SPI_ADDRESS "/dev/spidev0 .0"

Const unsigned char symb[16]=

{

 0b0011111, 0b00000110, 0b01011011, ob1001111,

 0b01100110, 0b01101101, 0b01111101, 0b00000111,

 0b01111111, 0b01100111, 0b01110111, 0b01111100,

 0b00111001, 0b01011110, 0b01111001, 0b01110001

};

Int transferData(int lg, unsigned char se, unsigned char rc[], int le)

Struct spi_ioc transfer trans;

Transfer.txx_buff = (unsigned long) se;

Transfer.rx_buff = (unsigned long) rc;

Transfer.le = le;

Transfer.speed_hez = 1000000; // speed in herz

Transfer.b_per_w = 8; // bits per word

Transfer.del_us = 0; // delay in micro second

Transfer.cx_change = 0; //chip affect transfer

Transfer.tx_nbits=0; //no bits for writing

Transfer.rx_nbits=0; //no bits for reading
```

```
Transfer.pd = 0; //interbyte delay

Int status = ioct1(lg, SPI_IOC_MESSAGE(1), &transfer);

If(status < 0)

{

  Perror ("*SPI: SPI_IOC_MESSAG Failed ");

Return -1;

}

 Return status;

}

Int main () {

 Unsigned int lg, I; //file to handle and loop counter

 Unsigned char null=0x00; // only sending one char

 Unit8_t mode = 3;    //SPI mode


 If (lg = open(SPI_ADDRESS, o_RDWR) <0 )

{

  Perror ("SPI Error: cannot open the device");

Return -1;

}

If (ioct1(lg, SPI_IOC_RD_MODE, &MODE)==-1)
```

```
{

Perror("SPI: Cannot set the mode of SPI");

Return -1;

}

If(ioctl (lg, SPI_TOC_WR_MODE, &mode)==-1))

{

  Perror("SPI: Cannot get the mode of SPI");

Return -1;

}

Printf("SPI Mode: %d\n", mode);

Printf("count in hexa from 0 to F");




For(i=0; i<=15; i++)

{

  // this code to receive and send the data

If(transfer(lg, (unsigned char*), &symb[i], &null, 1)==-1)

Perror ("cannot update the display");

Return -1;
```

```
}
```

Printf("%5d\r", i); //print the nun in the terminal window

fflush(stout); // flus the output

usleep(60000) // delay for 600ms in each loop

```
}
```

Close(lg);

Return 0;

```
}
```

You can use the ioctl() function to override the current settings of the device, but if you add xx you can read and write.

• SPI_IOC_XX_MOE: The transfer mode of SPI (0-3)

• SPI_IOC_XX_BITS_PER_WORD: determine the number of bits in each word

• SPI_IOC_XX_LSB_FIRST: 0 is MSB, 1 is LSB

• SPI_TOC_XX_MAX_SPEED_HZ: to set the max transfer rate in Hz

UART

UART stands for Universal Asynchronous Receiver/Transmitter. It's a microprocessor peripheral device that is used for serial data transfer, one bit at a time, between any two devices. UART was once a standalone IC, but it is now integrated with the host microcontroller. A UART is described as asynchronous because the sender can't send a clock signal to the recipient to synchronize the transmission. Usually the data is sent by only two lines such as your telephone line that uses the transmit data connection (TXD) and the receive data connection (RXD). It's very common to use the logic level for the UART outputs and inputs to enable two UARTs to connect with each other.

The number of symbols per second is called the baud rate, or modulation rate; the symbol could be two bits, so the byte rate will be $1/8^{th}$ of the bit rate.

This figure represents UART transmission format for one byte.

On the Raspberry Pi you will find the following:

A full UART that you can access via the GPIO header.

- TXD0 (pin8): to transmit data to a receiver

- RXD0 (pin 10): to receive data from a transmitter

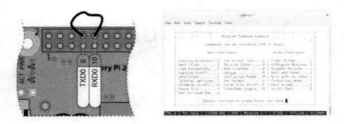

The /dev directory has an entry for ttAMA0. This is the terminal device, which is a software interface that enables you to send and receive data.

Advantages and disadvantage of UART communication

• Very simple wire transmissions with error checking, **but** the max data rate is very low compared to others like SPI.

• Easy to implement for interconnecting embedded devices and PCs, **but** the clock on both devices must be accurate especially at high baud rate.

• Can be interfaced to RS physical interfaces to enable long distance communication more than 15 meters, **but** you need to know the UART settings in advance like the baud rate, size, and checking type.

UART in C Programming

```
#include <stdio.h>

#include<fcnt1.h>

#include<unistd.h>

#include<termios.h>

Include<string.h>


Int main(int argc, char *argv[])

{

  Int myFile, myCount;
```

```
If(argc!=2)

{

Printf("please enter a string to your program\n");

Return -2;

}

If(myFile =open("/dev/ttAMA0", O_RDWR | O_noctty |
O_NDELAY) < 0 )

{

 Perror ("cannot open the device");

Return -1}

Struct termios options;

Tcgetarr(file, &options);

Options.c_cflag = b115200 | cs8 | CREAD | CLOAL;

Options.c_iflag = IGNPAR | ICRNL;

Tcflush(myFile, TCANOW, &options);

Tcflush(myFile, TCLFULUSH)

Tcsetattr(file, TCSANOW, &options);

If(count = write(myFile, argv[1], strlen(1)))<0)

{

Perror("UART: cannot write to the output\n");

Return -1;
```

```
}
```

Write(myFile, "\n\r",2);

Close(myFile);

Return 0;

```
}
```

In the above code we have used the termios structure.

The termios structure has many members:

- tcflag_t c_iflag: to set the input modes
- tcflag_t c_oflag: to set the output modes
- tcflag_t c_cflag: to set the control modes
- tcflag_t c_1flag: to set the local modes
- cc_T c_cc [NCCS]: Used for special characters

Questions for Chapter 7

1. Compare IIC and SPI.

2. Define UART.

3. Implement the UART in C.

4. List the advantages of SPI.

Chapter 8

Python Programming for the Raspberry Pi

What you will learn in this chapter:

Start programming with Python

Use Python for automation

Drive the hardware with Python

What you will need for this chapter:

Raspberry Pi board

Introduction to Python Programming

In this chapter you will learn how to use Python to develop basic encryption, user input, and graphical user interfaces.

Let's start with the "hello world" example as in any programming language.

Create a file named hello.py using the nano text editor.

Nano –c hello.py

Within the file write the following code:

#!/usr/bin/python3

#hello.py

Print ("Hello World")

After writing the code, save and exit. You can run the file using the following command:

Python3 hello.py

You should know more about strings if you want to start with Python.

A string is a sequence of characters stored together as a value. We will write code to get the user's input, using string manipulation to switch the letters and then print the encrypted message of the user input. You can use text editors that can be directly on your Raspberry Pi or via VNC or SSH. There are many text editors you can choose from:

• Nano: You can work with this editor from the terminal.

• IDLE3: This editor includes syntax highlighting and context help, but this program requires x-windows or x11 to run remotely. We will use Python 3, so make sure that you run IDL3 and not IDLE.

•Geany: This editor is an Integrated Development Environment (IDE) that supports many programming languages, syntax highlighting, auto completion, and very easy code navigation. This is a rich editor , but not for beginners and it will be slow on the Raspberry Pi. If you want to install Geany, write the following command:

 Sudo apt-get install Geany

To make sure that the Geany editor uses Python 3:

Click on the Execute button to run the code. You will need to change the build commands. Load the file.

Click build and set build commands and then change Python to Python 3.

Let's create the program

```
#!/usr/bin/python3

#ecryptionprogram.py

#takes the input and encrypt it

def encrpytText(input_text,key);

output=""""

for letter in input_text:

#Ascii Uppercase 65-90 lowercase 97 -122

Ascii_val = ord(letter)
```

```
#now write the following code to exclude non characters from
encryption

If(ord("A") > Ascii_val) or (Ascii_val > ord("Z")):

Output+=letter

Else:

#write this code to apply the encryption key

Key_val = Ascii_val + key

#make sure that we use A-Z regardless of key

If not((or("A")) < key_val < or("Z")):

 Key_val = ord("A") + (key_val-ord("A"))\

            %(ord("Z") –ord("A")+1)

#add the encrypted letter to the output

Output+=str(chr(key_val))

Return output

#Test

Def main()

Print ("please enter any text to encrypt")

#get user input

Try:

Us_input = input();

Sc_result = ecryptText(us_input, 10)
```

Print ("output: ", sc_result)

Print("to un-scramble , pls press enter")

Input()

Un_result = ecryptText(Sc_result, -10)

Print ("output: " + un_result)

Except UnicodeDecodeError:

Print ("this program supports ASCII characters only")

Main()

#end of the program

The preceding code implements a basic method to encode the text using a character substitution called the Caesar Cipher, named after Julius Caesar, who used this method to send his secret orders to the army.

We have defined two functions; encryptText() and main().

When the code is running, the main function contains the user's input using the input() command. The result is stored as a string in the us_ input variable.

Us_input = input()

● Keep in mind that the input() function can't handle non ASCII characters, so we will use try() function to solve this problem, which will cause UnicodeDecodeError.

We also call the encryptText() function with two parameters; the text to be encrypted, and the key. After that, the output will be printed.

Sc_result = ecryptText(us_input, 10)

Print("Output:" + Sc_result)

At the end, we will use input() to get the user input. The encryptText() will perform a simple form of encryption by shifting the position of the letters. That means substituting the letter with another letter based on the key; for example, if the letter is "A" and the key is 3 the output will be "D." This table shows you the idea of the Caesar Cipher.

In our example, "A" = 65, the key = 3, so the output = 65 +3 = 68 which is "D."

A	B	C	D	E	F	G	H	I	J	K	L	M
65	66	67	68	69	70	71	72	73	74	75	76	77
N	O	P	Q	R	S	T	U	V	W	X	Y	Z
78	79	80	81	82	83	84	85	86	87	88	89	90

After that, we will make sure that we have an empty string to build our result (output = ""), and then we will set our key to encrypt the text.

The input_text variable will contain strings that are stored as a list (a list is something like an array). You can access every item in the list using input_text[0] for the first item and so on. Python also allows you to loop through a list using the line of code for "item" in "items", to access each item.

The **letter in input_text**: This line allows you to break up the input by looping it through for each item inside and to set the letter equal to that, so if the input is equal to HELLO, it will run the code five times for H,E,L,L, and O. This allow you to read every letter separately, and then add the new encrypted letter to the output string.

The next line , if(ord("A) > Ascii_val) or (Ascii_val > ord("Z")):,

We write this line to check if the character we are looking at is not between A and Z, which means it is may be a number or a mark. In this case, the program will exclude the character from the encryption process (the output will not change).

If the letter is correct (between A and Z), you can add the value to our encryption key of 10 (Shifting 10 positions).

Input: A B C D E F G H I J K L M N O P Q R S T U V W X Y Z

Output: K L M N O P Q R S T U V W X Y Z A B C D E F G H I J

As you want the encrypted message to be much easier to write, you have a small output between A and Z, so if the letter starts with X, you want to wrap it and count from A. You can do this by writing the %(modulus) function, that gives you the remainder value of the input (if you divide a number by another number) if the number is 24, and if you add 10, you will get 34. The value of 34%26 (26 is the total number of the letters) is 8. Start from A until H.

In ASCII, the A is equal to the number 65, so you will remove the offset from the key_val and then add it once you have the modulus value. The next code makes sure that you limit the ASCII values to anything between A and Z:

#makes sure that you use A to Z regardless of key

If not((ord("A")) < key_val < ord("Z")):

Key_val = ord("A") + (key_val-or("A"))\

$$\%(ord("Z") -ord("A")+1)$$

If the entered value is not between the values for A or Z, then you will allow the value to wrap around (after calculating the modulus the total number of letters between A and Z, which is 26). This works if the key is larger than 26 and if you are counting in the opposite way, for example:

if the key was negative, the decryption key will be positive.

The following figure will show you the basic form of encryption, you will supply the method and the key to the one you want to read your message:

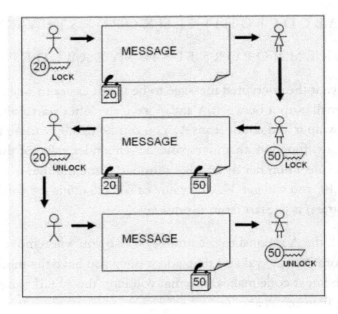

If you would like to send the message without the key and the method to the receiver, you will do the following as in the figure:

First, you will encrypt it and send the message over to the other one, and then they encrypt it again with their own encryption and send it back. The message at this point has two layers of the applied encryption. Now you can remove your encryption. At the end, the other side will receive the message with his/her encryption, which he/she can remove to read the message.

You should keep in mind that there are 25 encryption combinations.

You can run the file directly; Python will set _name_to the main global attribute with this code.

If __name__ =="__main__":

main()

Now let's create key.py and write the following code

```
#!/user/bin/python3

#key.py

Import encryptdecrypt as ENC

Key_1 = 20

Key_2 = 50

Print("enter your text: ")

#get user input

Us_input = input()

#send message

encodKey = ENC.encryptText(us_input, key_1)

print(us_1: send message encrypted with Key_1:" + encodKey)

encodKey2 = ENC.encryptText(encodKEY1KEY2, -KEY1)

print("us_1: removes KEY1 & returns with KEY2(KEY2):" +
encodKey2)

#Receiver will remove the encryption
```

Msg_res = ENC.encryptText(encodKEY2, -KEY2)

Print("us_2: will remove KEY2 & msg received :" + msg_res)

End of the program

Using files

In this part you will learn how to use and specify a file, via the command line, that will be read and encoded to produce the output file.

Now let's create a file named myFile.txt. Write the following code:

```
#!/user/bin/python3

#myfile.py

Import sys # to obtain command line parameters

Import encryptdecrypt as ENC

#define inputs

RG_IN = 1

RG_OUT = 2

RG_KEY = 3

RG_LEN = 4
```

```
def conv_File(in, out, key)

#convert the key to an integer

try:

encr_Key = int(key)

except ValueErr:

print("invalid: your key %s should be an integer" %(key))

#put it on to the lines

Else:

Try:

#open your files

With open(in) as f_in:

In_content = f_in.readlines()

Except IOError:

Print ("Unable to open %s" % (in))

try:

with open (out,'w') as f_out:

for line in in_content:

out_line = ENC.encryptText(line, enc_key)

f_out.writelines(out_line)
```

```python
except IOError:

print("cannot open %s %(in)")

try:

with open(out,'w') as f_out:

for line in in_content:

out_line = ENC.encryptText(line, en_key)

f_out.writelines(out_line)

except IOError:

print("cannot open %s" %(out))

print("the process is complete %s " %(out) )

finally:

print("complete")


#check the parameters

If len(sys.argv) == RG_LEN

Print("comm: %s" %(sys.argv))

convertFile(sys.argv[RG_IN], sys.argv[RG_OUT], sys.argv[RG_KEY])

else:

print("myFile.py in out key")

#End of the program
```

- To run the programs, write the following Python 3 myfile.py in the out key.

For instance, to encrypt myFile.txt and output it as encrypted.txt, use 20 as the key by writing the following command:

Python3 myfile.py in.txt encrypted.txt 20

If you want to show the result, use less encrypted.txt and enter Q to exit.

If you want to decrypt encrypted.txt and output it as decrypted.txt, use -20.

- Python myFile.py encrypted.txt decrypted.txt -20

This code requires us to use parameters that are provided in the terminal window. You will access them by importing the Python module called sys. Like you did before, you will also import your encrypt/decrypt module by the import command. You will use the part to allow you to refer to it using ENC.

Next, you will set the values to define what each command-line parameter will represent. If you run it , you will see that sys.argv[] is an array of values like in the following array:

['myfile.py', 'in.txt', 'encrypted.txt', '20']

So the input file will be at index 1 in the list, then the output file, and finally, the key with the total number of parameters RG_LEN = 4.

- Next, you will define the convertFile() function that you will call upon later from the next block of code.

- If you want to step away from errors, you will check if the length of the sys.argv value matches the number of parameters from the terminal window. This will make sure that the user has supplied you with enough, and you shouldn't try to reference items in the sys.argv[] list that don't exist. You will return a short message to explain what you are expecting.

- You will now call the convertFile() function via the terminal window values and making use of Python's built in exception handling features to ensure that errors are responded to accordingly.

- The line try/except code allow us to try to run some code and handle any exceptions (errors) in the program itself, and to halt any sudden stop.

The try code is accompanied by the following options:

- except valError: If an error occurs, a specific type of exception can be specified and handled with the action, depending on the error you wish to handle. For valError, you could check if the value is a float value and convert it to an integer or prompt for a new one. Multiple exceptions can be caught using except (valError, IOError) as required.

- except: This is to catch all cases of any possible exceptions that you have not dealt with. This point may the code be called from other places.

- else: This part of code is always executed if the try code is right and there is no exception, or any errors in the code will not be handled by the try/except block.

- finally: The finally part of code will always executed , even if there is no exception or if there is a problem with the try code.

- In other programming languages you will see something like try and except it, maybe try and catch, or also raise and throw as equivalents.

Let's create a boot menu, myMenu.py.

```
#!/user/bin/python3

#myMenu.py

From subprocess import call

FileN ="myMenu.ini"

DES=0

Key_k = 1

CM = 2

Print("Start Menu: ")

Try:

With open(fileN) as f:

myMenuFile = f.readlines()

except IOError:

print("cannot open %s" %(fileN))

for item in myMenuFile

line = item.split(',')

print ("(%s):%s" % (line[KEY_k], line[DES]))

#Get the user input

Run = True
```

While(run)

Us_input = input()

#check the input

For item in myMenuFile:

Line = item.spilt(',')

If(us_input == line[KEY_k]):

Print("comm:" + line[CM])

#run the script

Comm = line[CM].rstrip().split()

Print(comm)

Run = false

If len(comm):

Call(comm)

If(run == true):

Print ("your key in not exist in the menu")

Print ("everything is done")

Create a menu named menu.ini file that will contain the following:

Start Desk,d, starty

Show ip Address, I, hostname –I

Show cpu speed, s, cat /
sys/devices/system/cpu/cpu0/cpu/cpufreq/scaling_cur_

Freq

Show core temp, t, sudo /opt/vc/bin/vcgencmd measure temp

Exit,x,

• You can add your command and you can customize the list based on your needs..

If you want to execute any other programs from a Python script, you will need to use the command "call". You only wish to use the call part of the subprocess module, so you can simply use the subprocess import call.

• Open the file and read the lines in a menufile array. You can process each item as follows:

Line ['Start', 'Desk','d', 'starty']

You can access each section using the print statement separately, so you can print the key you need to press for a specific command and the description of the command.

Us_input == line[KEY_k]

The call command will require a command and its parameters to be a list, so you will use the split() function to break the command part into a list (every space in the statement will use the function).You should note that after\n is the end of the line character after starty, and this is the end of the line character from mymenu.ini. You will remove the first using the function rstrip() that is used to remove any whitespace.

Start:

Menu:

(d): start Desk

(i): Show ip Address

(s): show cpu speed

(t): show core temp

(y): exit

Using Python for automation

In this part, you will mainly work with the command line. You will also work with the Raspberry Pi by using a graphical user interface (GUI).

It will be very easy to get the input from the graphical user interface in a natural way. Python supports this. Much like any other programming language, you will use the Tkinter module that provides a lot of good controls and tools to create graphical user interfaces.

The app you will make is to convert the encryption application into a graphical user interface instead of using the command line.

Make sure that you have completed the instructions in the previous part; encryptdecrypt.py program

If you want to use Tkinter (one of add-ons of python), you will need to make sure that it is installed. By default it will be installed on the standard Raspbian image, but let's confirm that by importing it for a Python shell.

>>> import Tkinter

If it doesn't exist you will see an error (import error). In any case, you can install it using the command:

Sudo apt-get install python3-tk

If it did load , you will use the following command to read more:

>> help (tkinter)

Also, you can find a lot of information about the classes, functions and methods by writing the following command:

>>> help(tkinter.Button)

If you want to list any valid commands, you should write the following command in your shell:

>>> dir (tkinter.button)

Now let's use the tkinter to develop a GUI for the encrypt program:

```
#!/usr/bin/python3

#encrypt.py

Import encrypt as ENC

Import tkinter as TK

def encbutton():

encryptVal.set(ENC.encryptText(encryptVal.get(), keyVal.get))

def decButton():

encryptVal.set(ENC.encryptText(encryptVal.get(). –keyVal.get()))
```

```
#Tkinter application
Root =TK.TK()

Root.title("Enc/Dec application")
#control values
encryptVal = TK.StringVar()
enryptVal.set("this is a message")
keyVal = TK.IntVar()
keyVal.set(20)
promp = "Enter your message to encrypt: "
Key_k = "Key: "
Labl_1 = TK.label(root, text = promp, width=len(promp), bg='red' )
texEnter=tk.Entry(root, textvariable =encryptVal, width = len(promp))
encbutton = TK.Button(root, text="enc", command=encbutton)
decButton = TK.Button(root, text="dec", command=decbutton)
labl_2 = TK.label(root, textvariable=keyVal, width=9)
#Layout
Labl_1.grid(row=0, cloumnspan=2, sticky=TK.E + TK.w)
texEnter.grid(row=1, cloumnspan=2, sticky=TK.E+TK.W)
encbutton.grid(row=2, column=0, sticky=TK.E)
```

decbutton.grid(row=2, column=0, sticky=TK.W)

labl_2grid(row=3, column=1, sticky=TK.W)

TK.mainloop() #end of the program

In this program we start by importing modules

First one is the encrypt/decrypt file and the second one is the tkinter module.

The encbutton() and decbutton functions will be run when click on the encrypt and decrypt buttons

Now let's take a look at the code

Labl_1 = TK.label(root, text=promp, width=len(promp), bg='red')

All of the controls have to be linked to the window, you have to determine your tkinter window root. You will set the text using the text variable as shown. You have to set it to a string named promp that we defined previously with the text. You also can set the width to match the number of characters of the message, but it's not necessary to do that. You set the background color by using bg = 'red'.

In the next line of code, you defined the textEntry(root, textvariable=encryptVal, width=len(promp)), you also defined textvariable as a useful way to link variables to the contents of the box that is a string variable. You can access the text using textEnter.get() if you want, but this will allow you to separate the data you got it from the code which handles the graphical user interface. Use a Tkinter StringVar() to access it directly. The encryptVal variable used to update the Entry widget is linked to the .set() command.

Encbutton = TK.button(root, text=t"Encrypt", command=encButton)

decbutton = TK.button(root, text="decrypt", command=encButton)

In this case, you can set a function to call it when the button is pressed:

```
def encbutton():

encryptVal.set(ENC.encryptText(encryptVal.get(), keyVal.get))
```

Drive the hardware with python

One of the features of the Raspberry Pi is to set it from home computers; it has the ability to interface with any hardware.

The General purpose input – output (GPIO) pins can control a lot of low level electronics from LEDs to motors and displays.

Controlling an LED in Python

You will need:

- Female to male wire (4)

- Breadboard

- RGB LED

- 470 ohm resistors (3)

This figure show you the difference between the RGB LED and the other LED:

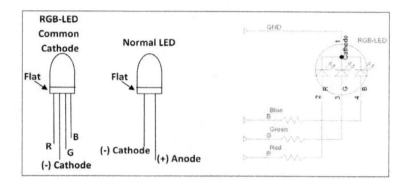

Controlling an LED in python (wiring)

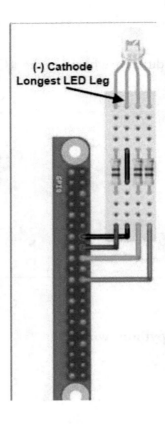

(-) Cathode
Longest LED Leg

Controlling an LED in Python (coding)

#!user/pin/python3

#led.py

```
Import RPi.GPIO as GPIO

import time

#RGB LED

# now setup the hardware

RGB_Ena = 1; RGB_Dis = 0

#LED Configuration

RGB_R = 16; RGB_G = 18; RGB_B=22

RGB = (RGB_R, RGB_G, RGB_B)

Def led_set():

#wiring

GPIO.setmode(GPIO.BOARD)

#ports

For val in RGB:

GPIO.setup(val, GPIO.OUT)

Def main():

Led_set()

For val in RGB:

GPIO.output(val, RGB_Ena)

Print("LED is on now ")

Time.sleep(7)
```

GPIO.output(val, RGB_Dis)

Print ("LED is off now ")

Try:

Main()

Finally:

GPIO.cleanup()

Print("Everything is closed now, the END")

#End of the program

Control the LED using a button (wiring)

You will need:

- **Female to male wires**

- **Breadboard**

- **Push button switch**

- **General purpose LED**

- **470 ohm resistors (2)**

- **Breadboard wire**

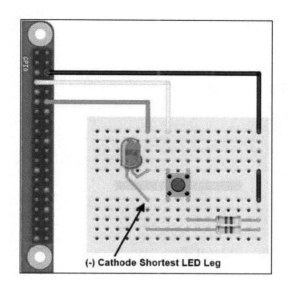

(-) Cathode Shortest LED Leg

Control the LED using a button (coding)

#!/usr/bin/python3

#control.py

Import time

Import RPi.GPIO as GPIO

Import os

#close the script

debugging = True

nd = True

#setup the hardware

118

```
#GPIO

#config

MODE = GPIO.BOARD

Sht_BIN = 7

LD = 12

Def gpio_Set():

#wiring

GPIO.semode(GPIO.MODE)

#ports

GPIO.setupt(sht_BIN, GPIO.IN, pull_up_down = GPIO.PUD_UP)

GPIO.Setup(LD,GPIO.OUT)


Def doShut():

If(debugging):print("you pressed the button")

Time.sleep(4)

If GPIO.input(Sht_BIN):

If(debugging):print("skip the shutdown (<4sec)")

else:

if(debugging):print("do you want to shut down the RPi NOW")

GPIO.output(LD,0)
```

```python
Time.sleep(0.6)

GPIO.output(LD, 1)

If(ND):os.system("flite –tWarning 3 2 1' ")

If (debugging == false):os.system("sudo shutdown h now")

If(debugging):GPIO.cleanup()

If(debugging):exit()


def main():

GPIO_set()

GPIO.output(LD, 1)

While True:

If(debugging):print("you can press the button")

If GPIO.input(sht_BTN)==False:

doShut()

time.sleep(2)

try:

main()

finally:

GPIO.cleanup()

print("every ting is closed now. The End")
```

```
#End of the program
```

Questions for Chapter 8

1. Using Python, create a file and put your name and your friends names into that file.

2. Design and develop an LED blinking system using a button and 3 LEDs.

3. Make the three LEDs blink in sequence order.

4. Design a graphical user interface to control the system in Question 3.

Chapter 9

Final Project

What you will learn in this chapter:

⚒Build a media center using the Raspberry Pi

What you will need for this chapter:

⚒Raspberry Pi board

⚒4 GB SD card or micro SD

⚒HDMI cable

⚒Ethernet cable

In this chapter you will build a media center on the Raspberry Pi board.

The first thing you will do is choose an operating system. I mean the appropriate operating system for the project because you will focus on making the Pi into a media center. There are two operating systems for this purpose; the first one is OpenELEC (Open Embedded Linux Entertainment Center), and the second one is OSMC(Open Source Media Center). In this project you will use the OSMC , so let's do the following:

- Download the OS.

- Install the OS on the SD card.

Download and Install the OSMC

Now you should choose the correct version of OSMC so you can download and install it. You can go to RaspberryPi.org, this is the official website for the Raspberry PI. As shown before in the past chapters, you can use this web site as a support community for you because you can share your experience the other Raspberry Pi users or read about theirs.

Now go to the main page and then choose DOWNLOADS. There, you will find a list of all the options of the operating systems you can choose from, or you can start working with Noobs that provide a look at what the Raspberry PI can do. You will find under these lists a third party operating system, and at this part you will find the OSMC, so just click on it.

- After completing the download, you can now install it. Make sure that you have the appropriate SD card that you can use on the

Raspberry Pi. If you don't have WinRAR, just go to the WinRAR website and install it and extract the image.

Now it's time to burn the operating system onto the SD card. Make sure that the file is ended with .img, then open the image burning program and burn it.

After burning the image on the SD card, you can set up everything now. You will need the following hardware:

The power supply

This power supply will make the difference to the Raspberry Pi, because if the pi is underpowered it will tell you it doesn't enough power during high-CPU usage.

Video – Audio Output

You can use the HDMI cable to connect your Raspberry Pi, but you should keep two things in mind: the length and the stiffness of the cable.

Internet Cable (Ethernet Cable)

You use this cable to connect you device to the Internet, but you can also use the USB Wi-Fi dongle.

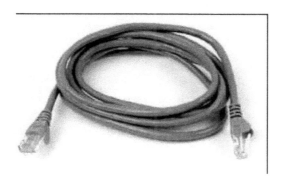

Now it's time to plug everything in:

● Plug the Raspberry Pi to the power supply and USB devices.

● Plug your preferred video/audio cable to either the HDMI or RCA ports.

● Hook the Raspberry Pi to the TV.

Start working with the OSMC

● This operating system uses a front end called Kodi. In this part you are going to become very familiar with the OSMC (Operating System Media Center), and you are going to do the following:

● Work and navigate the keyboard

● Start looking at the settings

● Set up and configure the network

Work and navigate with the keyboard

If you use your PC or your laptop, you may do most of your actions using the mouse to click on different menus or to open programs.

You mainly use your keyboard only when you enter your IP Address, typing something like an email, or playing a game. On the OSMC you can navigate with your mouse, but it will be much better than your keyboard and that depends on the version of your Raspberry Pi board.

The home screen of the OSMC:

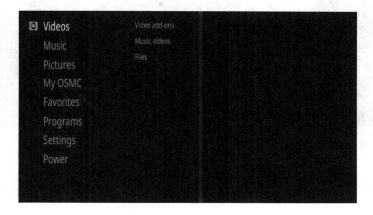

OSMC has a lot of different ways that you can use the content. I will show you how to stream it from different sources.

The Files menu is where videos can be found. We will discover how to get videos into the right place so you can watch them later. The most important thing you should know is the video add-ons. This is where Kodi comes in, and you will spend a lot of time adding new programs and watching your favorite videos.

Music

This screen is like the video screen. You can store your sounds or audio files if you open it from this screen. Like with videos , if you stored a collection of audio files somewhere, you can access it from the

OSMC from this screen as well. Also, you will find the music add-ons like the video add-ons.

The settings

In the settings, you can find the following info

129

• File manager: If you want to transfer something from a USB onto the Raspberry Pi like pictures or movies, you will open the directory from the file manager.

• System info: This will give an overview of the things running on the Raspberry Pi, and it also provides you with information like the IP address, summary, storage, memory, and so on.

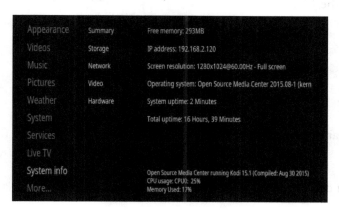

• Profiles: The profiles are something like the users on the Windows operating system; you add users, delete, and edit something like the privileges similar to any operating system.

MyOSMC

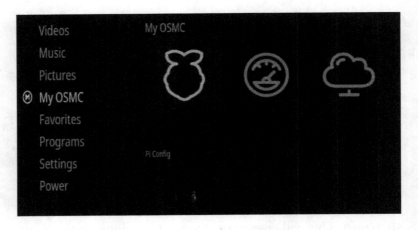

This screen handles hardware, overclocking, networking, and controls to connect the OSMC from another computer in case you want to transfer the file.

Wi-Fi

If you want to connect to the Internet wirelessly, you will use the Wi-Fi.

And you can set up it from this screen as shown:

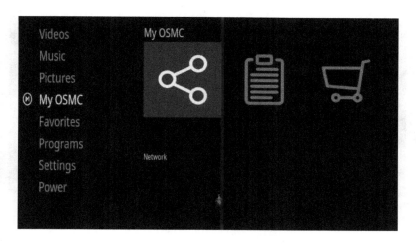

After plugging your Wi-Fi dongle and running your OSMC, you can go to the network and then click "Wireless." Click yes and finally apply.

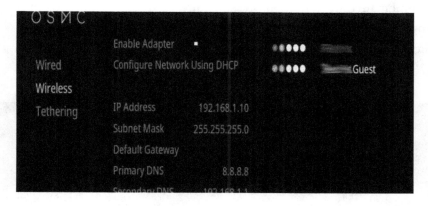

Install video add—ons

If you want to install new applications on the OSMC, you will navigate over to videos: Add-ons and press enter. Any apps(add-ons) that have been installed will be found here.

There are many choices you can choose from. You will scroll a long list of choices and take time to choose one. You can install it easily by dimming anything and then pressing enter, but you should look at the language of the app because the same app may have multilingual versions and you may prefer a specific one.

After installing a few apps , press backspace to see what apps you have installed.

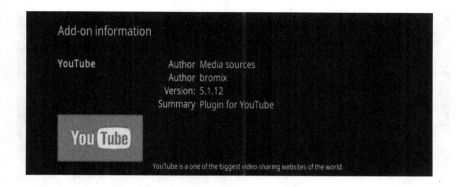

Music add-ons

If you interested in music you can also do the same thing. There are a lot of streaming options available that you can add on the Raspberry Pi. You can go to music by using the keyboard and pressing enter on music.

Videos   Files

♫ Music   Music add-ons

Pictures

My OSMC

Favorites

Programs

Settings

Move and copy your files

You will use now the file manager to copy or move files. From the main page, go to "settings" and then choose "file manager."

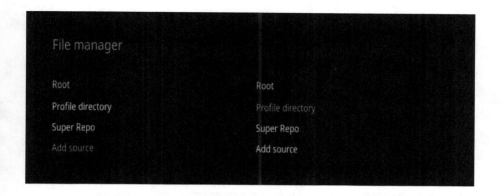

- In this figure you can see that there is a directory called Super Repo. If you plugged in your USB, you can see the directory listed on the file manager screen.

- After inserting your USB stick, scroll to your USB until you see your files and then copy any file you want. For example, llc.mp3, then go to any directory you want and paste it there.

- If you want to play the DVDs and ISOs , the Raspberry Pi can do that but you will need to do the following:

Get the codec, go back to www.raspberrypi.org

• Click on "shop" until you reach to the Raspberry Pi Swag Store and press on that. There are many categories like buy a Pi, Codecs, and so on.

• You will use codec/OS, so choose this.

• For DVDs, you will need an **MPEG-2 LICENSE KEY,** so you will purchase the codec and then press on the license "please click here to buy your mpeg-2 license key."

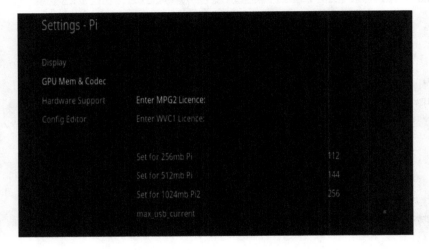

Go to MyOSMC from the main menu, then pi config, and finally to GPU Mem & Codec.

- Keep in mind that not all of the Raspberry Pi boards will process this code.

- If you want to play a DVD you will need to add an external DVD reader to the Raspberry Pi that you connect via USB to your computer.

Networking

- In this part you will learn how to connect your OSMC over the network.

- You should connect with computers in your home network.

- Everything you will do with your home network can be done with larger networks.

- Some of the benefits of connecting your OSMC is to watch your movies on TV, for example.

- You will focus on your home network instead of Raspberry Pi and OSMC.

Sharing in Windows

● You should remember how to share with Windows, Samba, and SMB.

● Sharing is one of the easiest things that you can do in Windows. After installing Windows , if you want to share a folder you can just click on it, choose "properties," and then click sharing.

Sharing in Linux

● If you are using the Linux operating system, you can use SSH (secure shell).

If you want to share your Linux computer and the OSMC, simply do the following:

Open the terminal window and then write this command:

Sudo systememct1 enable sshd

If your computer didn't process this command, don't worry.

You can try the other command:

Sudo service ssh start

And then write the following:

Sudo systememct1 start sshd

NFS (Network File Share)

- Network file sharing on Linux is something like the sharing in Windows..

- When you want to connect to a remote folder, your computer will be like a local folder.

- It will be more complex to setup the Network File Share than an SSH.

Because you will make the other users someone other than yourself, so you will need to set the permissions.

Sudo mkdir any name / nfs

Sudo shown user: user /nfs

Chmod 777 /nfs

Sudo nano /etc/exports

/nfs   *(rw)

Samba

This is the last option to share media from your Linux computer to OSMC, and it is Samba.

Now open the terminal window and write the following command:

Sudo nano / etc/samba/smb.conf

We can scroll down all the way and then add our information for the folder we are sharing.

[sharing name]

Path = /samba

Writable = yes

Guest ok = yes

Hosts allow = 192.168.

We can enable and start the Samba service.

Sudo systemct1 enable/start smb

Service smbd start

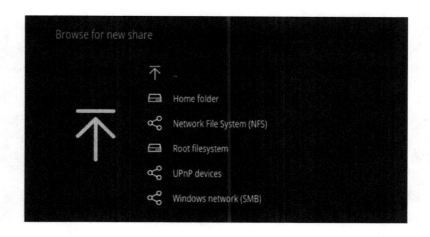

Browse for new share

⌃ ..

🖴 Home folder

⁂ Network File System (NFS)

🖴 Root filesystem

⁂ UPnP devices

⁂ Windows network (SMB)

www.ingramcontent.com/pod-product-compliance
Lightning Source LLC
Chambersburg PA
CBHW071102050326
40690CB00008B/1087